I0069927

GUIDELINES FOR PREPARING AND USING A DESIGN AND MONITORING FRAMEWORK

SOVEREIGN OPERATIONS AND TECHNICAL ASSISTANCE

OCTOBER 2020

ASIAN DEVELOPMENT BANK

ADB

Creative Commons Attribution 3.0 IGO license (CC BY 3.0 IGO)

© 2020 Asian Development Bank
6 ADB Avenue, Mandaluyong City, 1550 Metro Manila, Philippines
Tel +63 2 8632 4444; Fax +63 2 8636 2444
www.adb.org

Some rights reserved. Published in 2020.

ISBN 978-92-9262-386-9 (print); 978-92-9262-387-6 (electronic); 978-92-9262-388-3 (ebook)
Publication Stock No. TIM200275-2
DOI: http://dx.doi.org/10.22617/TIM200275-2

The views expressed in this publication are those of the authors and do not necessarily reflect the views and policies
of the Asian Development Bank (ADB) or its Board of Governors or the governments they represent.
ADB does not guarantee the accuracy of the data included in this publication and accepts no responsibility for any
consequence of their use. The mention of specific companies or products of manufacturers does not imply that they
are endorsed or recommended by ADB in preference to others of a similar nature that are not mentioned.

By making any designation of or reference to a particular territory or geographic area, or by using the term "country"
in this document, ADB does not intend to make any judgments as to the legal or other status of any territory or area.

This work is available under the Creative Commons Attribution 3.0 IGO license (CC BY 3.0 IGO)
https://creativecommons.org/licenses/by/3.0/igo/. By using the content of this publication, you agree to be bound
by the terms of this license. For attribution, translations, adaptations, and permissions, please read the provisions
and terms of use at https://www.adb.org/terms-use#openaccess.

This CC license does not apply to non-ADB copyright materials in this publication. If the material is attributed
to another source, please contact the copyright owner or publisher of that source for permission to reproduce it.
ADB cannot be held liable for any claims that arise as a result of your use of the material.

Please contact pubsmarketing@adb.org if you have questions or comments with respect to content, or if you wish
to obtain copyright permission for your intended use that does not fall within these terms, or for permission to use
the ADB logo.

Corrigenda to ADB publications may be found at http://www.adb.org/publications/corrigenda.

Notes:
In this publication, "$" refers to United States dollars.
The Asian Development Bank's Strategy, Policy and Partnerships Department is the source of all information in tables,
figures, boxes, and infographics in this report, unless otherwise stated.

Cover design by Cleone Baradas.

Updated from time to time, the guidelines in this publication describe how a project-level design
and monitoring framework should be developed and used throughout the project cycle for
sovereign operations and technical assistance projects.

For guidance specific to private sector operations, consult ADB's *Guidelines for Preparing and Using
a Design and Monitoring Framework: Private Sector Operations.*

CONTENTS

TABLES, FIGURES, AND BOXES

TABLES

FIGURES

BOXES

ABBREVIATIONS

ADB	–	Asian Development Bank
COBP	–	country operations business plan
CSO	–	civil society organization
DLI	–	disbursement-linked indicator
DMC	–	developing member country
DMF	–	design and monitoring framework
km	–	kilometer
M&E	–	monitoring and evaluation
MFF	–	multitranche financing facility
NA	–	not applicable
OP	–	operational priority
PAM	–	project administration manual
PAP	–	program action plan
PBL	–	policy-based lending
PCR	–	project completion report
PDMF	–	policy design and monitoring framework
PPP	–	public–private partnership
PPR	–	project progress report
PRF	–	program results framework
RAMP	–	risk assessment and risk management plan
RBL	–	results-based lending
RRP	–	report and recommendation of the President
SMART	–	specific, measurable, achievable, relevant, time-bound
TA	–	technical assistance
ToC	–	theory of change
TVET	–	technical and vocational education and training

I. The Design and Monitoring Framework:
A Tool for Managing for Development Results

These guidelines describe how the design and monitoring framework (DMF) should be developed and used throughout the project cycle for sovereign operations and technical assistance (TA). The DMF is the main tool the Asian Development Bank (ADB) uses for managing for development results at the project[1] and program levels and a core element of ADB's project performance management system.

Managing for development results is a management approach that supports better performance and greater accountability by applying a clear, logical framework to plan, measure, and manage a project with a focus on the intended development results. It is a process of continuously learning and taking evidence-based decisions to improve performance. By clearly identifying the intended results of a project in advance, regularly collecting information to assess progress toward them, and taking timely corrective action, the project team is better able to maximize achievement of sustainable development results for ADB's developing member countries (DMCs).

Formulating a quality DMF is an essential first step in the project management cycle. In this process, a project mission leader and team must understand the stakeholders and their problems and develop possible solutions into a manageable initiative. The basic steps in the project management cycle are as follows:

(i) Identify results (outputs and outcome) and the causal relationships between them.
(ii) Identify alignment with the broader thematic-, sector-, or country-level results (impact).
(iii) Identify the external factors that could influence success or cause failure (risks and critical assumptions).

(iv) Select indicators to measure performance, identify baselines, and decide on targets to be achieved.
(v) Implement activities to deliver outputs.
(vi) Measure and analyze data, and use them to assess project performance (monitoring and evaluation).
(vii) Report on results achievement and make project management decisions based on evidence of performance.
(viii) Learn about successes and failures and integrate the lessons back into the project cycle.

The DMF milestones are shown in Figure 1.

Preparing the design and monitoring framework. As the basic source of information about planned performance, the DMF plays a central role in ADB's project management cycle. All DMFs should be formulated through a participatory process (Section III) and reflect an approach and format suitable to the modality or product type (Section IV). A preliminary DMF is attached to the concept paper for all projects including knowledge and support TA. Although the level of detail it contains will vary depending on how far project planning has progressed, the preliminary DMF includes at least an indicative impact statement and results chain, and general ideas for performance indicators. The target and baseline values for these indicators may not yet be determined. The DMF is fully developed and confirmed during the fact-finding stage and the finalized DMF is attached to reports and recommendations of the President (RRPs). DMFs for all projects are entered into ADB's web-based portfolio management system, "e-Operations," once the project has been prepared and before it is approved by the ADB Board of Directors.

---

[1] The term project is used throughout these guidelines as a general reference to all types of ADB operations.

Figure 1: Design and Monitoring Framework Milestones

DMF MILESTONES	Preliminary DMF drafted and refined	ADB- and DMC-agreed DMF completed	DMF monitored, reported on, and revised if needed	Final DMF reported on and used to inform evaluation	
PROJECT CYCLE PHASE	Identification, Design and Preparation	Approval	Implementation and Monitoring	Completion	Post-completion Evaluation
DOCUMENTS AND ACTIVITIES	• Concept paper • Reconnaissance and fact-finding missions	• RRP and TA report • Project administration manual	• Inception and review missions • Project performance report • Midterm review • Change requests	• Completion report	• Validation of completion report • Project and other special independent and self-evaluations

ADB = Asian Development Bank, DMC = developing member country, DMF = design and monitoring framework, RRP = report and recommendation of the President, TA = technical assistance.

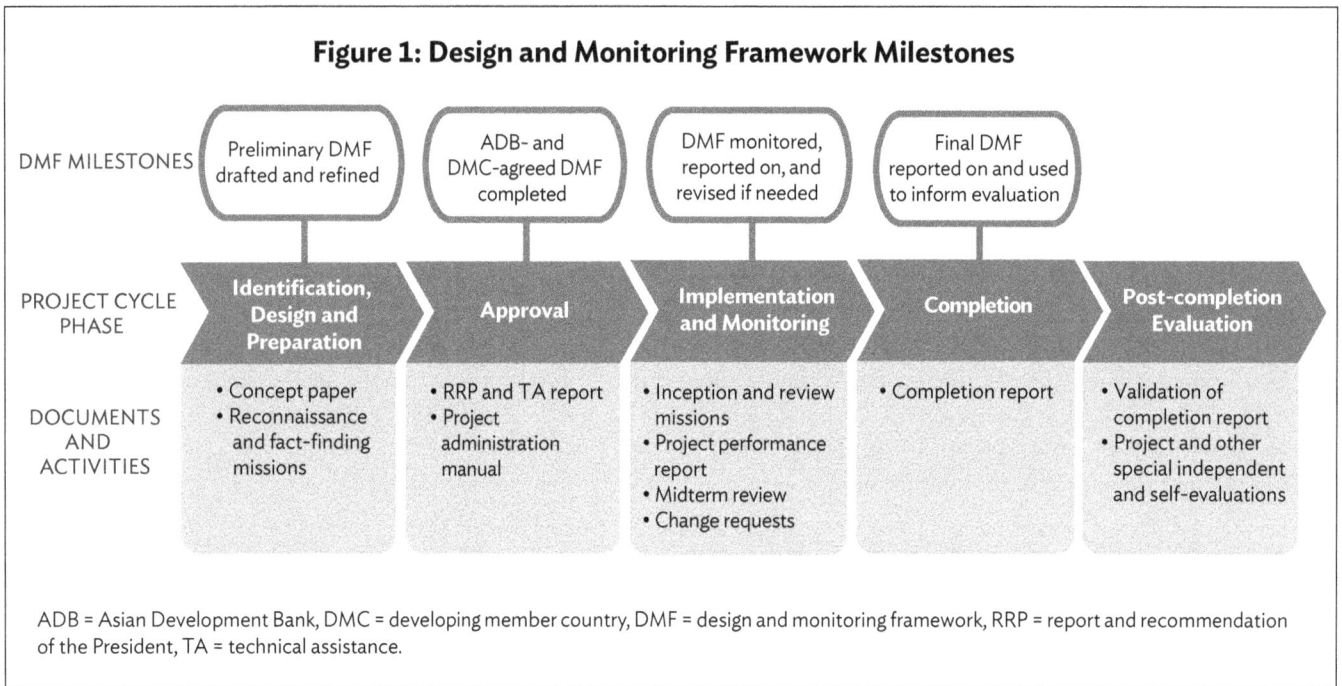

Using the design and monitoring framework during project implementation. Facilitated by the project's monitoring and evaluation arrangements (Section V.A), progress on DMF performance indicators is tracked and reported on regularly in e-Operations as part of project performance reporting. The DMF is updated throughout the project cycle to reflect all pertinent changes to the project following the procedures in the project administration instructions. If the project scope changes, the degree to which the DMF must be changed determines the approval authority required (Section V.B). If the DMF is updated, the e-Operations DMF records must reflect the changes.

Using the design and monitoring framework after project completion. The DMF forms the basis of the completion report for all operations and TA projects that require a DMF in their approval report, and project success is evaluated and rated against the DMF results chain and performance indicators (Section V.C).

II.   Design and Monitoring Framework Structure

The DMF captures critical information about the project in four columns (Figure 2). The top row of the DMF may contain a maximum of three impact statements with which the project is aligned. For sovereign projects, these statements are typically derived from a regional, country, or sector strategy. The four columns contain

(i)   the results chain, including the inputs, or main resources; the activities or groups of tasks; the outputs delivered by the project; and the outcome it will achieve;
(ii)   performance indicators for measuring results achievement, targets to be achieved, and a baseline of current performance;
(iii) data sources and reporting mechanisms for each indicator; and
(iv)   the risks that act against results achievement, and critical assumptions that underly the results chain.

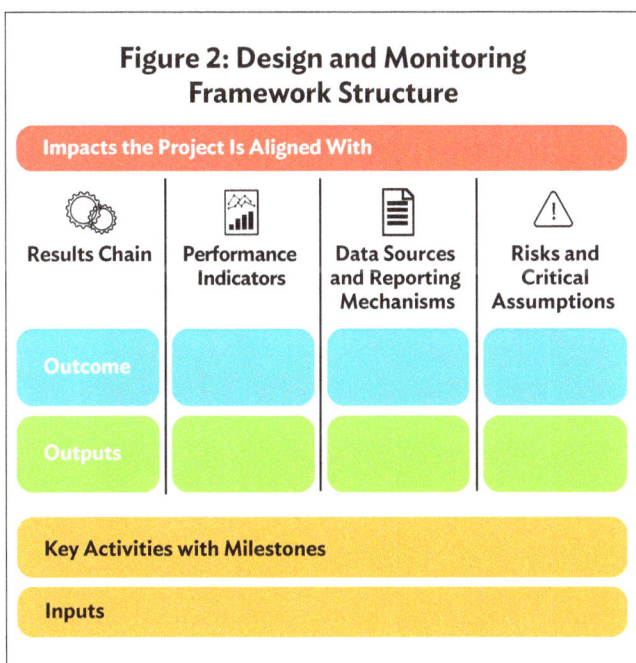

Figure 2: Design and Monitoring Framework Structure

Impacts the Project Is Aligned With

Results Chain	Performance Indicators	Data Sources and Reporting Mechanisms	Risks and Critical Assumptions
Outcome			
Outputs			

Key Activities with Milestones

Inputs

A.   Results Chain

The primary purpose of a project is to achieve results that meet people's and/or organizations' needs. A results chain consists of a series of expected achievements, or positive changes, linked by causality. The results chain is a continuum from inputs to activities to outputs, and to outcomes. Outputs are defined as goods, services, or products delivered by the project, while outcomes are the immediate and direct benefits of the use or application of the outputs. The following are important pointers for developing a results chain.

(i)   The alignment points for a project's results chain are impact statements, which are typically higher-level country, sector, or thematic results to which the project contributes. The impact statement aligns the project's outcome with a higher-level development result.
(ii)   The basic definitions and impact alignment are illustrated in Figure 3 using the example of an urban rail transit system project. The project delivers the following outputs: signaling, train control, and telecommunications systems operational; rolling stock operational; and institutional capacity of metro operations organizations strengthened. The immediate and direct benefit for residents of City A, the ultimate intended beneficiary group, is affordable, safe, and inclusive mobility of urban rail-based transit users in City A enhanced—the outcome. This outcome is aligned with the higher-level impact of improved connectivity for all to social and economic opportunities in City A.
(iii) The importance of the results increases moving up the results chain: efficient, safe, and inclusive transit is more important than an operational metro system, which is just a means to that end; and connectivity for all to social and economic

opportunities is more important still. However, project control and accountability decrease moving up the results chain. The project controls train system construction and capacity building, but it only influences the efficiency, safety, and inclusiveness of the rail-based urban transit system. The project is accountable for output delivery and outcome achievement, but not for impact-level results. Attribution also decreases from output to outcome to impact. The outputs and outcome are attributable to the project. The impact statement of connectivity for all to social and economic opportunities in City A is outside the project results chain and, although the project contributes to it to some degree, is not controlled by or attributed to the project.

Table 1 illustrates the differences between the results levels. It contains several concepts, including targets

risks and assumptions for partner financing, which are discussed in subsequent sections of these guidelines.

Outputs. Outputs are the products and services that the project delivers to the beneficiaries. Outputs are usually tangible and are generated by using and transforming inputs through project activities. The management scope of the project is defined by the outputs, as by definition, project management cannot extend beyond outputs. There is a close relationship between inputs and outputs; therefore the DMF cannot list outputs for which there are no inputs (Box 1). Before project approval, project teams assign a percentage weight for each DMF output indicator—based on its criticality to achieving and/or contribution to the project's outcome, cost, or other priorities—and input these into e-Operations. The percentage weights form part of ADB's project performance rating methodology used during project implementation.[2]

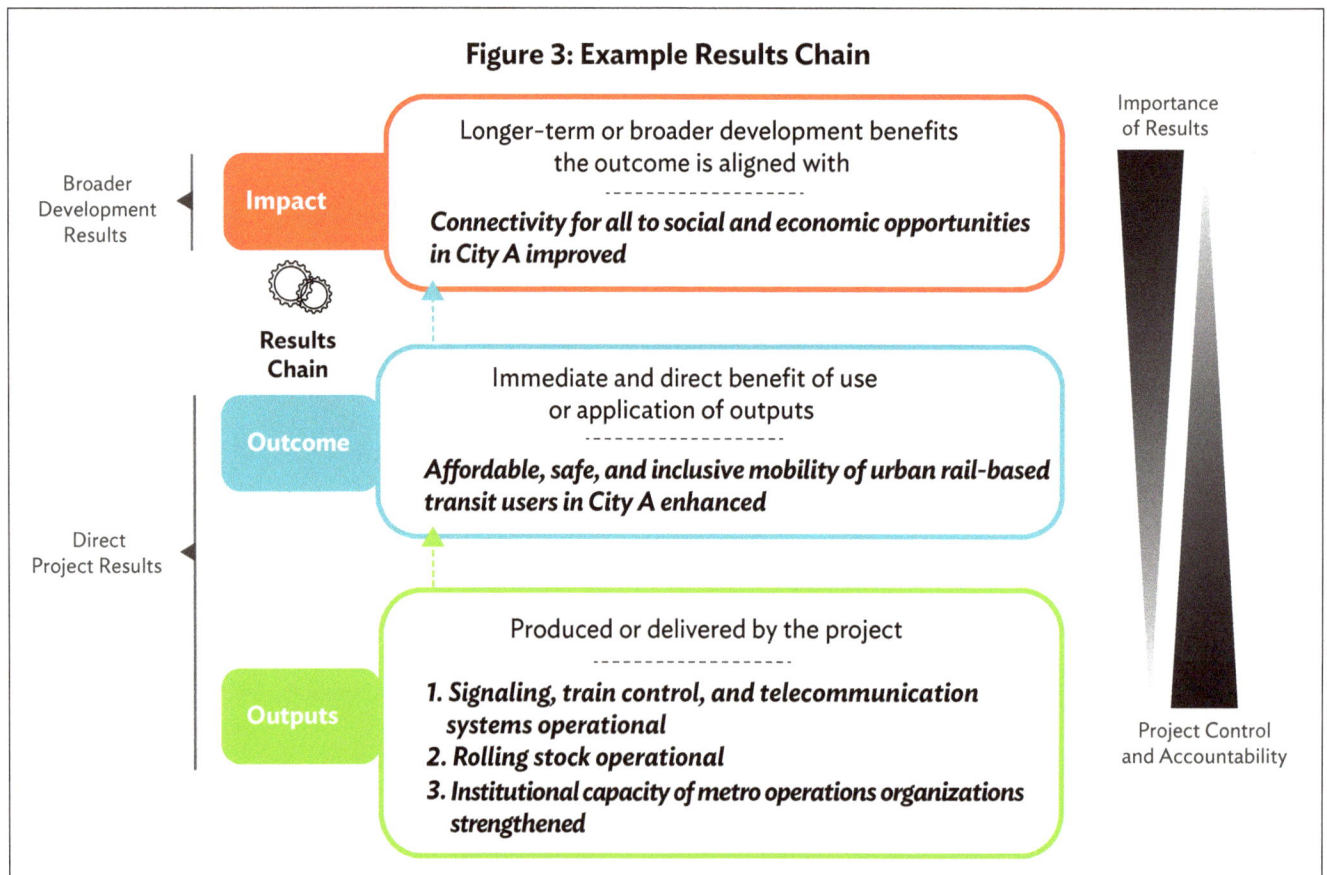

Figure 3: Example Results Chain

Broader Development Results

Impact

Longer-term or broader development benefits the outcome is aligned with
- - - - - - - - - - - - - - - - - - -
Connectivity for all to social and economic opportunities in City A improved

Results Chain

Outcome

Immediate and direct benefit of use or application of outputs
- - - - - - - - - - - - - - - - - - -
Affordable, safe, and inclusive mobility of urban rail-based transit users in City A enhanced

Direct Project Results

Outputs

Produced or delivered by the project
- - - - - - - - - - - - - - - - - - -
1. *Signaling, train control, and telecommunication systems operational*
2. *Rolling stock operational*
3. *Institutional capacity of metro operations organizations strengthened*

Importance of Results

Project Control and Accountability

---

2 ADB. 2020. Project Performance Monitoring. *Project Administration Instructions.* PAI 5.08. Manila. https://www.adb.org/documents/project-administration-instructions.

Table 1: Differences between Results Levels

Results Level	Relationship to Project	Source of Result	Timing of Achievements	Control by Project or Beneficiaries	Accountability	Changes during Project Implementation
Impact (not part of results chain)	Aligned with project outcome	Higher-level documents, e.g., national, sector, subnational, or regional plans or strategies	Usually post project	Outside beneficiary control	No direct project accountability	Should not change, although additional impact statements can be added to reflect alignment with a new strategy or plan introduced after project approval
Outcome (part of the DMF results chain)	Directly influenced by project	Needs of beneficiaries	Target level achieved by end of first full year of operation following physical completion, or before financial closure of project	Within the control of beneficiaries	Project accountable for outcome achievement Project success (effectiveness) measured against outcome targets	Major change in scope if there is a material change in the outcome
Output (part of the DMF results chain)	Produced or delivered by project	Project deliverables	By physical completion	Within control of project, given inputs, risks, and critical assumptions	Project accountable for outputs	Minor change in scope if no effect on the outcome

DMF = design and monitoring framework.

DMF Structure

Box 1: Output Tips

(i) Include major products and deliverables of the project.

(ii) Ensure that together, outputs will be sufficient to achieve the outcome, given the risks and assumptions.

(iii) Include an output for each set of activities, except project management activities, which do not produce an output.

(iv) Phrase outputs in the past tense as already achieved, e.g., "rural roads constructed in the southern districts." Include a word signifying completion (e.g., constructed, rehabilitated, established, implemented, improved) in the statement.

(v) Outputs must be fully consistent with the cost estimates and financing plan, and the project definition in schedule 1 to the loan or grant agreement.

Outcomes. Outcomes represent the purpose of the project and should describe the immediate and direct benefits of output use or application. Outcome statements should articulate the change the project is expected to achieve (Box 2). The DMF contains only a single outcome statement, although the statement may contain several different dimensions of performance, such as "Improved water security and mobility in City A." Performance indicators are then used to measure specific dimensions of the project outcome (Section II.B). For example, if women's mobility is an important part of the outcome, this dimension would be measured through a specific performance indicator.

Box 2: Outcome Tips

(i) Include only one outcome statement describing the immediate and direct benefits from using or applying outputs.

(ii) Phrase the outcome in the past tense as already achieved, e.g., "increased mobility of rural residents." The statement must include at least one change word (e.g., increased, improved, enhanced).

(iii) Do not include any cause-and-effect links. Outcome statements should not use the words "through," "by," or "in order to," because these words imply cause-and-effect links; e.g., corporate performance improved through capacity building, graduation rates increased by reducing dropouts, crop yields improved in order to increase farmer income.

Assessment of the project's effectiveness is based on whether the project's intended outcome has been achieved and is attributable to the achieved project outputs. For sovereign operations, the project completion report (PCR) is prepared within 12 months of financial closing. To ensure that outcome performance data will be available in time for completion reporting, the DMF articulates the planned level of outcome indicator target achievement in the first full year of operation following physical completion.[3] For projects with nonphysical outputs, the outcome indicator target dates should be set to ensure that achievement can be assessed in the PCR.

Impacts. The project's results chain is aligned with impact statements, which are sourced from the most relevant strategic document(s), usually a government national, sector, subnational, or regional plan or strategy, before the project is conceptualized. The impact level in the DMF is separated from the results chain to show that its purpose is alignment, not performance measurement. The DMF does not include performance indicators or targets to measure impact statements.[4] Impacts are long-term in nature and are expected to occur sometime after project closing. The timing of expected impacts varies. For example, a project that takes 6 years to build new transmission lines would make some contribution to the growth of businesses that use electricity only after several years of operation.

Impact statements are restated from the source document to conform to DMF results statement phrasing. Phrase the impact as achieved, for example, "income, jobs, and business activity increased" and include a change word in the sentence. Do not include more than one level of cause-and-effect links in an

---

[3]   A sovereign project is deemed complete when all of its outputs are completed (i.e., when its facilities are completed and ready to operate regardless of the closure of its financial account). Project Administration Instruction 6.07A provides instructions on the timing of PCR preparation and circulation (ADB. 2019. Project Completion Report for Sovereign Operations. *Project Administration Instructions.* PAI 6.07A. Manila). https://www.adb.org/documents/project-administration-instructions.

[4]   Although impact-level indicators are not included in the DMF, rigorous impact evaluation can still be carried out using the impact statement(s) and results chain from the DMF. See ADB. 2017. *Impact Evaluation of Development Interventions: A Practical Guide.* Manila. https://www.adb.org/sites/default/files/publication/392376/impact-evaluation-development-interventions-guide.pdf.

impact statement. Be careful not to choose an impact statement that is too high-level, such as "inclusive economic growth achieved" or "poverty reduced." A statement of this nature is too general to show alignment with the project. In rare cases where there is no relevant official document to cite or paraphrase (e.g., for some knowledge and support TA projects or in the case of disaster and emergency response projects), the impact(s) can be exclusively defined by the project and "(project defined)" is stated after the impact statement. In other cases, the second and third impact statements can be "project defined."

Table 2 contains output, outcome, and impact statements for operations in common ADB areas of sovereign programming.

The DMF includes two other levels: activities and inputs (Figure 2).

Activities. Activities are the groups of tasks carried out using project inputs to produce the desired outputs. The DMF should only include activities whose completion represents important milestones that will allow implementation progress to be tracked. For example, key activities for an education project might include "develop science, technology, engineering, and mathematics curricula and train trainers by Q4 2023"; "provide relevant training equipment to five selecting technical training institutes by Q3 2022"; and "develop and implement an in-service training program for teachers by Q4 2024."

Table 2: Example Results Statements for Operations in Common Areas

Results Level	Urban Transport	Energy Generation	Urban Water Supply	Training of Technical and Vocational Education and Training Teachers	Financial Intermediation
Impact (Long-term end goal, not part of results chain)	Jobs and economic activity increased	Health, education, jobs, and economic activity increased	Waterborne diseases reduced	Workforce skills and productivity increased	Employment in small and medium-sized enterprises increased
Outcome (Immediate and direct benefit of output use)	Travel convenience, safety, and affordability for women and men improved	Consumption of electricity in remote communities increased	Consumption of clean, treated water increased	Quality of technical and vocational education and training (TVET) delivery enhanced	Economically viable small and medium-sized enterprises, managed by women and men, increased
Output (Provided or delivered)	Urban rail system constructed Institutional capacity of Department of Transport strengthened	Off-grid solar energy installations constructed Capacity of residents in remote communities to use and maintain solar energy installations enhanced	Water distribution and treatment facilities in urban areas rehabilitated Institutional capacity of water utility service provider strengthened	TVET teacher knowledge and skills improved Quality and relevance of TVET curriculum improved Technical training institutes upgraded	Financing to microfinance beneficiaries, including women, through intermediaries increased

It is good practice to include project management activities at the end of the activities section of the DMF. The cluster should be titled "project management activities." The activities should summarize routine events and activities of the project implementation team or unit, such as planning, procurement, monitoring and evaluation, and reporting. Activities can also include communicating with stakeholders, providing inputs on strategic and policy issues, and undertaking risk mitigation measures. This cluster can help mission leaders organize project management activities and ensure that key project management concerns are budgeted for. There is no output associated with the project management activities, so they should not be numbered (Box 3).

Inputs. Inputs are the main resources that the project uses to undertake the activities and produce the

---

Box 4: Input Tips

(i) Include a summary of the main financial inputs needed to carry out the activities.

(ii) Group inputs by financier.

(iii) Include direct cofinancing.

(iv) For technical assistance, also include in-kind contributions by source (except for regional technical assistance).

---

outputs. All financial inputs, as well as in-kind inputs for TA, that will be used for project activities should be listed in the DMF. This includes those from ADB, the government, cofinanciers, beneficiaries, the private sector, and civil society organizations (CSOs), as applicable (Box 4).

Include all cofinancing administered by ADB (fully or partially), and cofinancing not administered by ADB but for which ADB and the financing partner jointly finance the same contract packages, as an input in the DMF with corresponding outputs. Cofinancing should be listed as a critical assumption in the DMF if a third party will finance, and deliver in parallel through separately administered procurement packages, outputs that are necessary to achieve the outcome (Section II.D1).

B. Performance Indicators

Results achievement is measured through performance indicators, which include targets to define success. Indicators clarify the expected results and determine their status using quantitative or qualitative measures (Box 5). Performance indicators provide a measurable basis for project monitoring and evaluation. Key stakeholders should be involved in the selection of indicators and targets to ensure these are ambitious yet realistic and reflect the needs of the intended beneficiaries.

Box 3: Activities Tips

(i) List key activities for each output.

(ii) Link design and monitoring framework activities with "B. Overall Project Implementation Plan" in Section II of the project administration manual.

(iii) Show the completion date and milestone for each activity.

(iv) Group and number activities by the output they relate to.

(v) Include project management activities as appropriate, such as procuring goods, hiring consultants, reporting, monitoring, evaluation, accounting, and auditing, at the end of the activities row, without a number.

(vi) Include any primary data collection undertaken for the project under project management activities.

(vii) Do not include indicators at the activity level.

(viii) For results-based lending, activities should be priority actions from the program action plan. Policy-based lending does not require activities.

Box 5: Tips for Measuring Quality Quantitatively

All indicators should be specified in quantitative terms. However, this does not mean that qualitative measurement cannot take place. Beneficiary satisfaction with government service is inherently qualitative and measures can be expressed quantitatively. For example, a quantitative indicator could be "Share of residents satisfied or highly satisfied with solid waste management services increased to at least 80% by 2025 (2020 baseline: 56%)." This indicator captures a qualitative dimension but expresses it in quantitative terms.

Existing indicators should be used where possible to reduce the time and costs required to collect data. This includes indicators for which data are already collected by government agencies, academic institutions, CSOs, and other sources. However, guard against selecting an indicator solely because it already exists. The primary function of the indicator is to measure the result; if the result is not being measured by an existing indicator, a new indicator must be developed.

There are three main types of indicators.

(i)   **Direct indicators** directly measure the subject of interest. For example, the number of fatalities from road accidents annually is a direct indicator of the outcome statement "reduced deaths from road traffic accidents." They are ideal indicators and should be used whenever feasible.

(ii) **Proxy indicators** are indirect measures that approximate to, or are representative of, the subject of interest. They are used to demonstrate change or results where direct measures are not feasible. For example, landlessness or poor housing quality may be used as proxy indicators of poverty. A proxy indicator may be used because (a) the subject of interest is qualitative and cannot be measured directly (e.g., living conditions or good governance); (b) the subject cannot be measured within the available resources or timeline (e.g., behavioral

change); and/or (c) it is better value for money to use a proxy indicator because a high-quality one exists.

(iii) **Leading indicators** measure preliminary indications of an outcome by measuring progress along the pathway of change. They provide evidence of something that typically needs to hold true or to occur for the desired outcome to be achieved but are not direct evidence of the outcome itself. For example, the number of workshop participants indicating their willingness or ability to apply the new skills they have learned is a leading indicator for their actual application of the skills.

1.   Selecting Performance Indicators

S	M	A	R	T
Specific	Measurable	Achievable	Relevant	Time-bound

Example

Journey from city station A to city station W by public transport reduced to less than 1 hour by 2025 (2020 baseline: at least 2 hours).

Each indicator must have a baseline and a target. The baseline is the most recent status of performance, while the target represents the expected level of achievement. All indicators must be specified quantitatively, as in the following example: Journey from city station A to city station W by public transport reduced to less than 1 hour by 2025 (2020 baseline: at least 2 hours).

A good performance indicator meets the "SMART" criteria.

(i)   **Specific**—details the outputs or outcome the project seeks to achieve by specifying dimensions, such as who, where, when, quality, quantity, and cost.
   • Be specific about who is benefiting by including details, as relevant, of beneficiaries' sex (male/female), location (urban/rural),

socioeconomic status, ethnicity, age, and any other relevant qualities. Ensure indicators that count people are always sex-disaggregated (Box 6).

- Ensure relevant stakeholders understand the indicator. Avoid subjective terms such as "access" or "successful." Instead, define exactly how the output or outcome will be measured. For example, instead of "education management information system (EMIS) successfully in use by Ministry of Education," use "Ministry of Education uses education management information system (EMIS) to generate regular quarterly reports."

(ii) **Measurable**—stated in quantifiable terms (e.g., percentage of children) and feasible to collect data in time to report in the PCR and in project progress reports as relevant.

- Use indicators that are industry standard for the sector or issue if available and practical.

Box 6: Measuring Progress in Gender Equality

Each Asian Development Bank (ADB) project is classified into one of four gender mainstreaming categories. One of the requirements for a project to be categorized *gender equity as a theme* is that its design and monitoring framework must have an explicit gender equality and/or women's empowerment outcome statement, and/or gender-specific outcome-level performance indicators, with at least 50% of outputs including proactive gender targets. Projects categorized *effective gender mainstreaming* must include performance indicators with proactive gender targets for at least 50% of outputs. Projects are categorized *some gender elements* if they include some proactive gender targets. Projects that do not meet these requirements will be categorized *no gender elements*.

Source: ADB. *Guidelines for Gender Mainstreaming Categories of ADB Projects.* Manila (updated from time to time).

- Where possible and appropriate, use indicators for which data are already collected, but do not use an indicator solely because it already exists. If there is no preexisting relevant indicator, seek to identify an indicator for which data can be collected using information systems that are already in place.
- Keep in mind that collecting new data may require data collection activities that have an added cost. These should be planned and budgeted for.

(iii) **Achievable**—realistic about what is to be achieved. The collective judgment of key stakeholders is needed to choose a target that is ambitious, yet realistic. (E.g., is a 1-hour reduction in travel time on public transit from city station A to city station W by 2025 realistically achievable?)

(iv) **Relevant**—appropriate to the results statement it measures and useful for management information purposes. (This requires management judgment: will knowing the public transit journey time from city station A to city station W be useful for managing the project or assessing its success?).

(v) **Time-bound**—stated with a target and baseline, both with dates (e.g., 1 hour by 2025; 2020 baseline: 2 hours).

To be specific, indicators should measure and express quantitatively various dimensions of a result, as follows:

(i) **Quantity**—how much of the result has been delivered? (e.g., number, percentage, ratio)

(ii) **Quality**—with what quality? (e.g., client satisfaction percentage, quality rating scale, pass/fail, yes/no, error rate, design standards or features in the case of outputs)

(iii) **Timeliness**—when, according to set schedule, and for how long? (e.g., by calendar date, length of time, number of hours to use the service)

(iv) **Location**—where are the results located geographically? (e.g., village, state, region)

(v) **With whom**—which groups are involved? (e.g., ethnic groups, women, people living below the poverty line)

(vi) **Cost**—at how much cost per unit? (e.g., $ per child immunized, $ per kilometer [km], $ per application processed)

2. Collecting Baseline Data and Setting Targets

Baseline data should reflect the most recent status of performance. If a project starts in 2022, the baseline data should be for the most recent year, ideally 2021. Transaction TA or knowledge and support TA can be used to collect baseline data. Figure 4 shows the relationship between target, performance, and baseline.

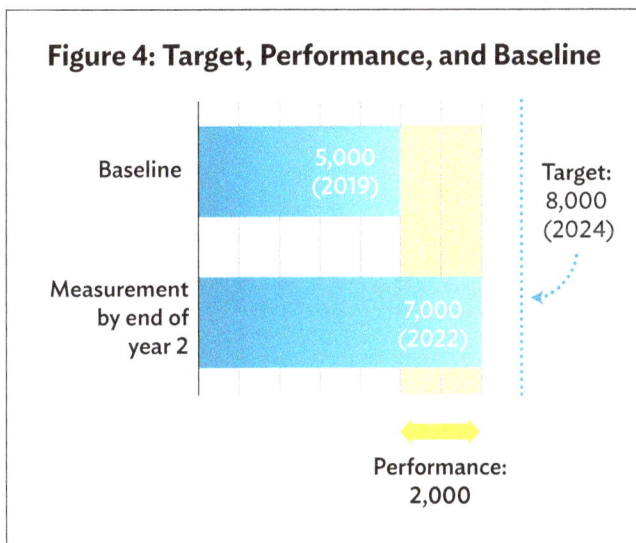

Figure 4: Target, Performance, and Baseline

All indicators must have one of the following four types of baselines.

(i) **Cumulative baselines** are usually used for outcomes in which additional units will be added to an existing stock or when existing performance can be measured; for example, "Share of residents satisfied or highly satisfied with solid waste management services increased to at least 80% by 2025 (2020 baseline: 56%)."

(ii) **Zero baselines** are usually used for outputs when a project is starting from nothing and adding units; for example: "250 km of road upgraded by 2025 (2020 baseline: 0 km)."

(iii) **Binary baselines** are usually used in policy-based lending (PBL) when something is to be adopted, approved, or operationalized; for example, "transport master plan for capital city adopted by city council in 2022 (2020 baseline: drafted)." This type of baseline is recorded quantitatively in e-Operations as 0 and its associated target, once achieved, is recorded as 1, hence the term "binary."

(iv) **Not applicable** (NA) is used for outputs or outcomes when a result is the first of its kind, there is nothing to measure against, and the baseline does not exist; for example, "100% of proposals reviewed by investment board by 2023 (2020 baseline: NA [investment board does not exist yet])"; or "at least 95% of workshop participants report improved knowledge of e-procurement platform by 2025 (2020 baseline: NA [e-procurement platform not yet developed])."

Each indicator must have quantitative targets. Targets should be set taking into account the needs of stakeholders; the baseline; and, if available, benchmarks of comparative performance. If an indicator measures more than one dimension of performance, it will need a baseline and target value for each dimension. For instance, in the following example, both the rural and urban dimensions of performance have a separate baseline and target: "24-hour power supply provided for 100% of urban population and 85% of rural population by 2026 (2020 baseline: urban 65%, rural 53%)."

Output and outcome targets must be quantitative, but they do not have to take a single numerical value. They can be set using a range of options, as shown in Table 3. Box 7 provides tips on formulating performance indicators with targets.

Table 3: Options for Target Setting

Target Type	Examples	Key Features	Use When:
1. Numerical	Average speed along North–South roadway increased to 60 kilometers per hour by 2026 (2020 baseline: 20 kilometers per hour average).	A point target that is expected to be reached or exceeded	A precise level of performance can be expected
2. Maintained or increased Maintained or decreased	Level of nitrous oxides in urban air maintained or decreased by 2026 (2020 baseline: 90 micrograms per cubic meter).	A floor or ceiling for desired performance in reference to the baseline	The current level of performance is satisfactory, performance improvements are also desirable, but no target amount can be set
3. At least	Staff with malaria prevention accreditation increased to at least 90%, 100% for female staff by 2026 (2020 baseline: 78%, 55% [female]).	A floor for desired performance that does not reference the baseline	A minimum level of target performance can be set and the desired performance trajectory is upward
4. No more than	Road accident response time reduced to no more than 20 minutes by 2026 (2020 baseline: 60 minutes).	A ceiling for desired performance that does not reference the baseline	A minimum level of target performance can be set and the desired performance trajectory is downward
5. On time or on schedule	By 2023, annual audited financial statements published online by 15 July (2020 baseline: at least 6 months late).	A point target that is set with reference to a future date or time	Expected performance is time- or calendar-based
6. Maintained	By 2024, annual operation and maintenance cost recovery maintained at 2019 level (2019 baseline: 105%).	Baseline performance is to be sustained A range can also be specified, e.g., 100%–130%.	The current level of performance is satisfactory and no improvement is expected

Box 7: Tips for Performance Indicators

(i) Include at least one indicator for each output and outcome. No indicators are included in the design and monitoring framework for impacts.

(ii) Align the indicator directly with the output or outcome. Ensure that the indicators do not measure the next or previous level of results and that together they measure all dimensions of the corresponding results statement.

(iii) Use stakeholder input where appropriate, especially from beneficiaries, to specify indicators and set targets.

(iv) State the baseline for each dimension of performance measured by the indicator: current performance level, zero, or not applicable.

(v) Specify a target for each dimension of performance measured by the indicator using one of the six target types. Disaggregate any indicator that measures people into female and male for baselines and targets, and ensure targets are supported by the findings of the gender analysis.

(vi) Specify indicators quantitatively, even if measuring qualitative dimensions.

(vii) Limit the number of indicators by including only "need to know" indicators and avoiding "nice to know" indicators.

(viii) Use relevant existing indicators where possible, but ensure timely data will be available for monitoring and reporting.

C. Data Sources and Reporting

For each performance indicator, the DMF must record (i) the title of the report or document that will contain the data about the indicator; (ii) the name of the issuing organization; and (iii) how frequently the data will be made available (e.g., monthly, annually, biennially) (Box 8). For websites, state "website data" and footnote the website address. For indicators that require primary data to be collected by the project, also record the data collection method or tool in the DMF; for example, "survey of workshop participants" or "survey of beneficiary households" (Box 9).

Primary data are those that are collected by the project itself. Secondary data have already been collected by a third party, such as a government department, academic institution, international organization, or CSO. The data collection activities required to collect primary

Box 8: Tips for Data Sources and Reporting

(i) Be as specific as possible about the data source and reporting mechanism. Simply noting "project completion report" is almost always too general. The appropriate data source is critical for collection of valid, quality data; and the design and monitoring framework is meant to be instructive and helpful to those responsible for data collection and reporting.

(ii) For all indicators, include the document name, author, and frequency of publication.

(iii) Number each data source or reporting mechanism to correspond to the applicable indicator.

(iv) Budget for each primary data collection process. Include outcome-level primary data collection, or primary data collection for new indicators, under project management activities.

(v) Data collected about beneficiaries should be disaggregated at least into male and female, and other groups as relevant.

Box 9: Tips for Common Data Collections Methods

There is no single best way to collect or retrieve data. The most appropriate data collection method is one that yields the most valid and credible data for the indicator and is feasible given resource availability and time constraints. For some indicators, it may be worth collecting the data using more than one method or source to cross-verify the findings and yield more detail, greater accuracy, and thus validity. Consult subject-matter experts and key stakeholders when choosing methods. Common data collection methods for design and monitoring framework indicators include the following:

(i) **Reviews of existing official documents and data.** This includes sources such as management information systems, administrative data, and official statistical databases.

(ii) **Observation.** This involves direct observation or assessment by a qualified expert or experts; for example, the level of participation by women in official meetings is observed and assessed by a gender specialist; the application of skills on the job is observed and assessed by a supervisor.

(iii) **Information from individuals or groups.** This includes key informant interviews, focus group interviews, or a panel of experts; surveys (web-based, handwritten, or verbal face-to-face); and mobile data collection. These are ideally administered both pre- and post-project. They can also be administered once at the end of the project; in which case they need to include questions that reconstruct the baseline if no comparable baseline data already exist.

(iv) **Physical measurements.** Methods in this category are based on agreed indicators and measurement procedures and include measuring geographical information or biophysical changes (e.g., incidence of flooding, incidence of illness, or pollution levels).

data, such as conducting a survey of beneficiaries, should be included in project management activities and budgeted for. The timing of primary data collection and the responsibility for undertaking it must also be determined. These roles, responsibilities, and associated deliverables should be detailed in the project administration manual and consultants' terms of reference.

Primary data can be collected using a range of methods, including document or administrative data review, interviews, focus group discussions, surveys, expert panel advice, on-site observation, analysis of web-based or digital data, and equipment readings.

When developing a data collection strategy there are several factors to consider in determining what to measure and how to measure it, including representativeness, bias, and attrition. For further guidance, consult *Impact Evaluation of Development Interventions: A Practical Guide.*[5]

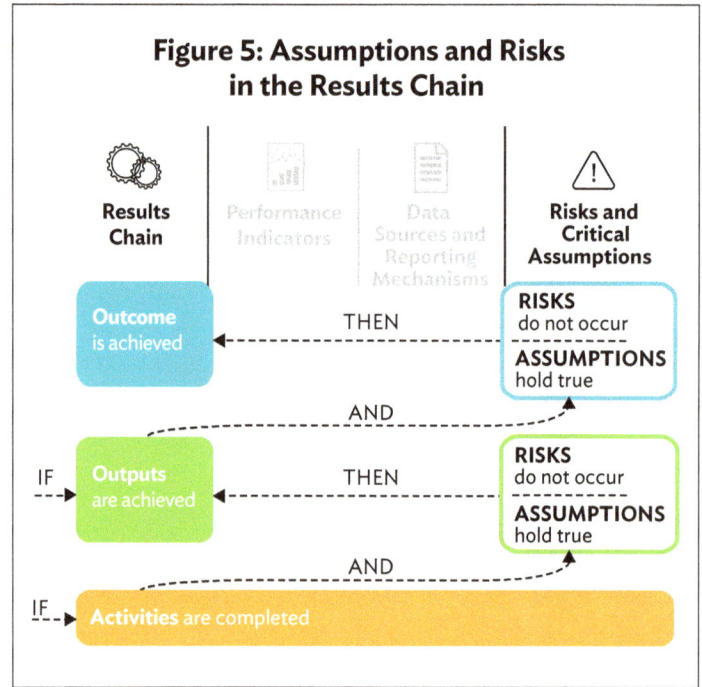

Figure 5: Assumptions and Risks in the Results Chain

D. Assumptions and Risks

The outputs and outcome depend to some extent on economic, political, social, behavioral, financial, environmental, and institutional factors for their achievement. These factors can be classified as assumptions or risks and should be included in the DMF if they critically affect the results chain.

Good project design involves identifying clear, valid assumptions and risks. Assumptions and risks fill in the cause-and-effect gaps between results levels; they fit between the activities and outputs, and outputs and outcome. Figure 5 depicts the logical sequence of assumptions and risks in the results chain. A useful approach for thoroughly identifying assumptions and risks is to build out the project's theory of change (ToC) (Section III.D).

Registering assumptions and risks in the design and monitoring framework. The DMF should contain at least one critical assumption or risk at the outputs level, and at least one critical assumption or risk at the outcome level.

Assumptions vs. risks. The processes for identifying critical assumptions and risks are similar in that they involve asking the question "what conditions or factors might prevent the project from achieving the desired results?" However, a risk is not simply the negative restatement of an assumption. The distinction between the two concepts is summarized in Figure 6, which includes illustrative examples of a potential critical assumption and a risk for a project aiming to reduce urban air pollution by installing clean heating systems in city households. It would be relevant to include in the DMF either the critical assumption or the risk illustrated in Figure 6, but not both.

1. Assumptions

Assumptions are the positive conditions, events, or actions that are expected to occur, although not with 100% certainty, and are required for the achievement of the project's planned results. All project results chains are based on assumptions. The higher up the results chain, the more assumptions there are.

---

[5] ADB. 2017. *Impact Evaluation of Development Interventions: A Practical Guide.* Manila. https://www.adb.org/sites/default/files/publication/392376/impact-evaluation-development-interventions-guide.pdf.

Figure 6: Assumptions vs. Risks

Risks and Critical Assumptions

RISK

A negative condition, event, or action that could jeopardize achievement of desired results; low to high probability of occurrence.

- - - - - - - - - - - - - - - - - - - -

Climate-related disasters may force an increase in migration into City A at a rate beyond projections that outpaces delivery of clean household heating systems.

(A relevant risk if there is a low to high probability it will occur and its occurrence would substantially jeopardize the project's success.)

ASSUMPTION

A positive condition, event, or action that must be in place for the project to achieve desired results. Very high probability, but not 100%, of occurrence.

- - - - - - - - - - - - - - - - - - - -

Migration rates into City A remain consistent with or lower than projections.

(A relevant assumption if evidence plausibly demonstrates that it is highly probable.)

Positive for results achievement

RISK	ASSUMPTION

Unlikely to happen ◄──────────────► Likely to happen

RISK	RISK

Negative for results achievement

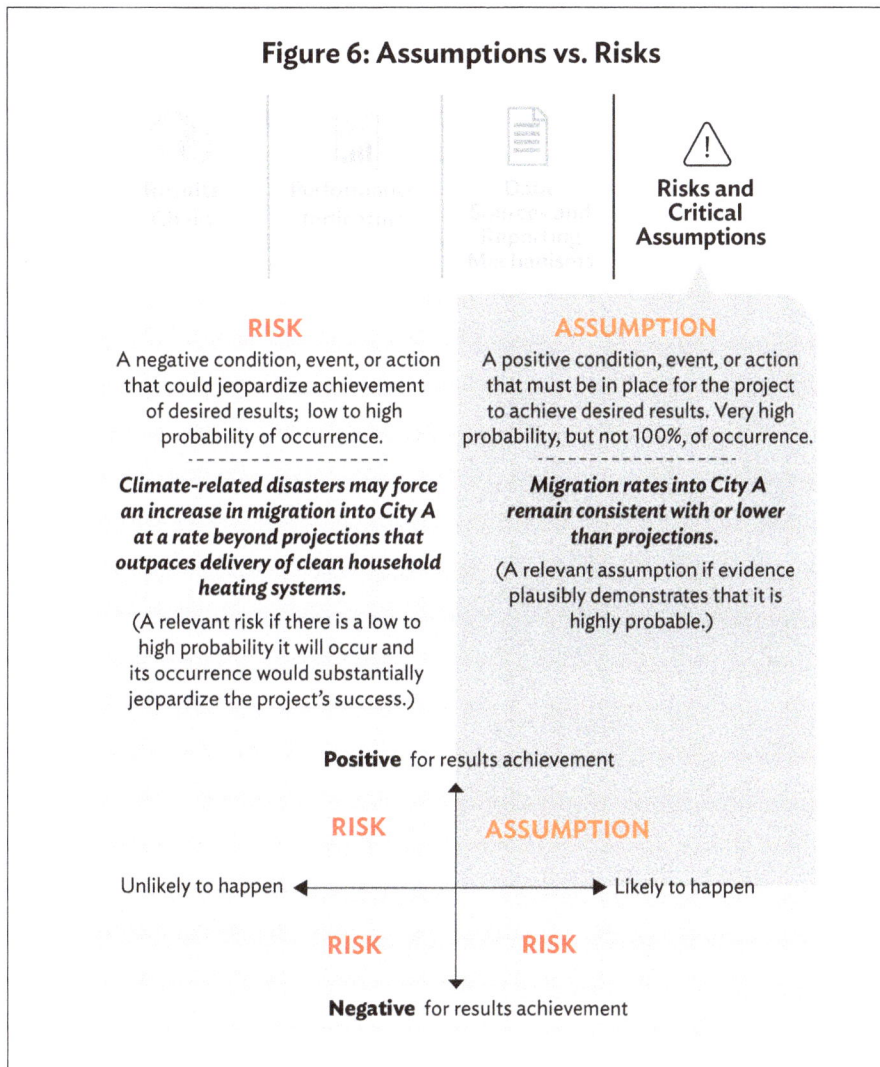

This is because project stakeholders have a higher level of control and influence on inputs, activities, and outputs than on outcomes and impacts. When an assumption fails to hold, results may be compromised. Analyzing and stating critical assumptions can improve project design by helping identify additional inputs, activities, or outputs that should be included in the project design to best ensure it achieves development results and to set output and outcome targets that are realistic. Analyzing assumptions also helps identify project risks.

Identifying assumptions. Assumptions can be divided into two general types: external factors, including assumptions for partner financing, and those relating to the internal cause-and-effect logic of the project's results chain. To identify assumptions, consider the following questions:

(i)   What are we assuming will happen for our planned activities to lead to our outputs, and for our planned outputs to lead to our desired outcome?

(ii)   What conditions must be in place to achieve our desired results? Of these, which are we unsure will be in place in time to achieve the desired results?

External assumptions. Often, assumptions relate to the context within which key project stakeholders will work to achieve targeted results. For example, most ADB-supported projects are designed under the assumptions that there will be continued economic, social, climatic, and political stability within the project environment, and government priorities will remain unchanged over the planning and implementation periods. As these are general assumptions that apply to most projects, it is not helpful to include them in the DMF. However, each of these general types of external assumptions merits closer consideration by the project team to identify project-specific critical external assumptions that warrant inclusion in the DMF; for example, related to climatic and social stability, "migration rates into City A remain consistent with or lower than projections" (Figure 6).

Assumptions for partner financing. Parallel cofinancing that is not administered by ADB is an important factor outside the project's control that often helps achieve the outcome. For example, an ADB-supported water project may install a piped water distribution system (output) but not the household connections (second output) needed for households to use the treated water. However, another development partner may be providing financing to connect households. If the outcome of the ADB-supported project is "household consumption of treated water increased," the ADB-supported project outputs, together with the outputs financed by the other partner(s), should be sufficient to achieve this outcome. When these other outputs are not administered by ADB, are financed in parallel, and are needed for the ADB-supported project to reach its outcome, they should be recorded as an assumption in the DMF along with the name of the financier. For example, "World Bank Group installs water supply connections to 250,000 households."

Assumptions about the internal cause-and-effect logic of the project's results chain. These important links implicit within the project's results chain often relate to human behavior or the technical feasibility of project plans. For example, a project for which the output statement is "teachers' skills improved" and the outcome statement is "students receive improved quality of teaching" assumes that the teachers trained will subsequently be willing and able to apply what they have learned in the classroom. This assumption is a critical link in the pathway of change between the project's outputs and outcome. These types of assumptions merit questioning because the project should be designed to rely on the smallest number of critical assumptions possible. Critical assumptions about the internal cause-and-effect logic of a project's results chain should be based on evidence. Evidence should be cited in the RRP, with clear reference to studies and comparable contexts in which the cause-and-effect logic has been demonstrated.

Registering critical assumptions. Assumptions for partner financing must be identified in the DMF. Including any other assumptions critical to project success is optional. An assumption is considered critical when the project will probably not work as planned and may fail to achieve its intended results if the assumption does not hold true in reality. Figure 7 provides a decision tree to help identify critical assumptions. In addition to identifying critical assumptions in the DMF, it is good practice to identify and explain them in the section of the RRP that describes the project's design and include them as conditions in loan covenants, as relevant, to ensure they hold true.

2. Risks

Risks are factors that can hinder progress from one results level to the next. They are potential conditions, events, or actions that would adversely affect, or make it difficult to achieve, the outputs and outcome, or to sustain the outcome. For sovereign operations, all risks are recorded in the risk assessment and risk management plan (RAMP), a linked document to the RRP.[6] Risks assigned ratings of *high* or *substantial* in the RAMP and whose occurrence would have a significant

---

[6] The RAMP is a mandatory linked document in Appendix 2 of the RRP. OM C4/OP states that the RAMP should address the public financial management, procurement, and corruption risks based on the preliminary assessment in the project concept paper. (ADB. 2019. Operations Manual Bank Policies. *Operations Manual*. OM C4/OP. Manila. https://www.adb.org/documents/operations-manual.). TA projects do not require a RAMP unless they involve specific governance or procurement risks.

Figure 7: Decision Tree for Identifying Critical Assumptions

Risks and Critical Assumptions

AN ASSUMPTION

? Is the assumption important for achieving project objectives?

NO → Leave out

YES

? What is the degree of certainty that this assumption will hold true?

CERTAIN → Leave out

LESS LIKELY → Likelihood of it holding true is too low to be a critical assumption. Identify barriers to this assumption holding true and include them in risk analysis.

HIGHLY LIKELY → Include and monitor

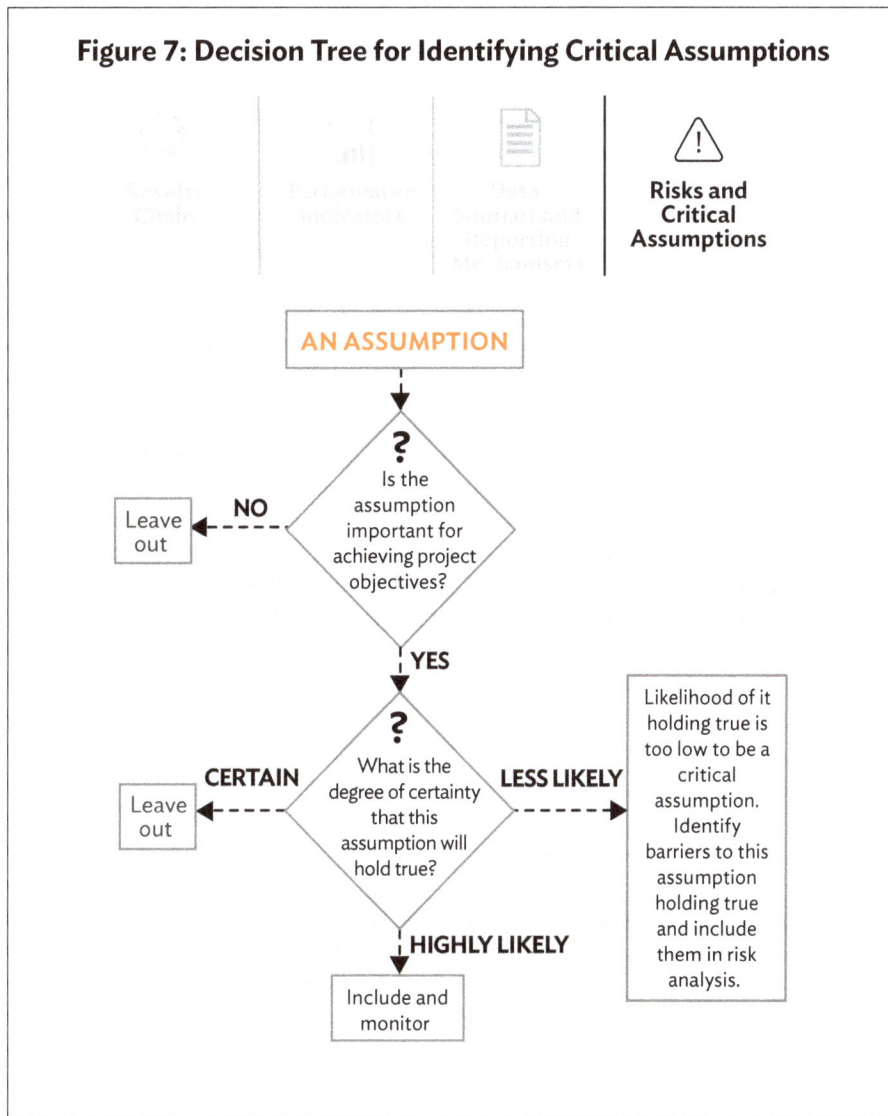

negative effect on achievement of the outputs or outcome are stated in the DMF.

Identifying risks. To identify risks, consider the following questions:

(i) What are the forces acting against project success?

(ii) What occurrences or actions might happen at any point in the project cycle that would significantly jeopardize achievement of the intended results?

For example, critical factors affecting the outcome "mobility of people and goods between cities A and B increased" include deteriorating security conditions, adverse weather events beyond projected parameters, and deterioration of economic conditions decrease ability to pay for transport. The analysis would be as follows:

(i) Are security conditions necessary to increase mobility? Yes. Are they likely to remain stable or improve? No. State as risk: "Security conditions in rural areas deteriorate."

(ii) Would adverse weather events beyond projected parameters affect mobility? Yes. Are they likely to happen? Yes. State as risk: "Storm season is worse than projected."

(iii) Is the decreased ability to pay likely to constrain mobility? Yes. Is it likely to happen? Preparatory studies show that people are able and willing to pay for transport, but there is a medium degree of likelihood that the country will enter a recession in the coming years, which if it happens, would reduce poor people's ability to pay for transport. State as risk: "Deterioration of economic conditions decreases ability to pay for transport."

A risk should satisfy two conditions to be included in the RAMP: its occurrence must be uncertain, and if it occurs it should negatively affect the achievement of project results. For example, "security conditions" is not a risk; the current state of security is a known fact with no uncertainty. However, "security conditions deteriorate" is uncertain and therefore a possible risk. The RAMP should be updated throughout the course of project preparation. Any measure taken or planned that puts a risk within the project's full control, or removes the uncertainty about it, also changes that risk to a fact, which should then be removed from the RAMP. A risk that is included as a loan covenant or a project readiness criterion, or is eliminated by project redesign, should not be included in the RAMP because it has been brought within the project's full control.

Analyzing risks. An analysis of risks is important to understand the constraints the project may face. Some risks may be important enough to warrant action to mitigate their potential effects. Others, referred to as "killer risks," may require the project to be redesigned or not undertaken. Figure 8 shows a risk analysis matrix that can be used to categorize risks and select appropriate actions.

Depending on the importance and/or likelihood of the risks occurring, the following actions can be taken.

(i) *Low:* Accept risk, take no action.

(ii) *Moderate:* Periodically measure the risk factor, especially for changes in likelihood of occurrence.

(iii) *Substantial* and *high:* To the extent possible, mitigate effects through design (Box 10). Include

design measures to reduce the likelihood of occurrence or the effects if the risk occurs and create a contingency plan to be ready to deal with the consequences of the risk occurring.

(iv) *Killer risk:* Redesign the project.

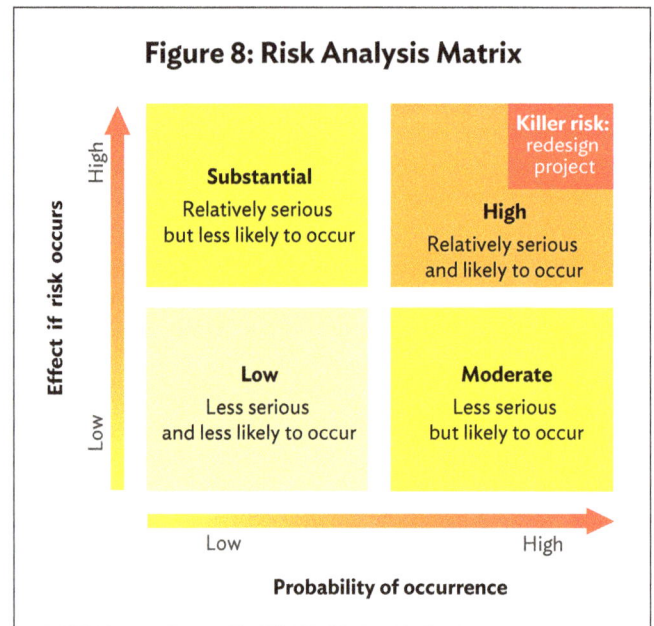

Figure 8: Risk Analysis Matrix

Effect if risk occurs

High

Substantial
Relatively serious but less likely to occur

Killer risk: redesign project

High
Relatively serious and likely to occur

Low

Low
Less serious and less likely to occur

Moderate
Less serious but likely to occur

Low　　　　　High

Probability of occurrence

Box 10: Mitigation Tip

Mitigation refers to actions undertaken to reduce or remove the effects of a risk occurring, or the likelihood of occurrence. Mitigation does not remove the risk. The project can only remove the risk through redesign. Not all risks can be mitigated, and when they cannot and the project moves forward, their possible effects are accepted.

Registering risks. For sovereign operations, all major risks to the project are identified and analyzed in the RAMP. Rate each risk in the RAMP as *high, substantial, moderate,* or *low.* List all *high* and *substantial* risks from the RAMP in a table in the RRP. From this table, identify all risks that would affect achievement of the outputs or outcome and that fit within the vertical logic of the results chain, and include these in the DMF (Box 11).

Box 11: Risk Tips

(i) Risks are negative and uncertain.

(ii) Do not include as risks (a) any factors that the project fully controls, (b) risks included as loan covenants, (c) project readiness criteria, (d) risks already eliminated through redesign, and (e) planned mitigation measures.

(iii) For sovereign operations, list all project risks in the risk assessment and risk management plan. List all *high* and *substantial* risks from the risk assessment and risk management plan in the summary of risks and mitigating measures table in the report and recommendation of the President.

(iv) In the design and monitoring framework, list all *high* and *substantial* risks that would affect achievement of the outputs or outcome and fit within the vertical logic of the results chain. Risks can be linked to specific outputs if desired.

(v) Risks that would threaten delivery of outputs, even if all activities were successfully completed, are listed at the output level in the design and monitoring framework; while risks that would threaten achievement of the desired outcome or its sustainability, even if all outputs were successfully delivered, are listed at the outcome level.

3. Monitoring Critical Assumptions and Risks

Risks and critical assumptions should be monitored closely throughout project implementation. During review missions, project teams should review the risks that may affect the likelihood of achieving DMF targets, reassess the executing and implementing agencies' capacity to mitigate these risks, and document any updates in the back-to-office report and aide-mémoire.[7] When a planned result is not achieved or problems occur, a faulty assumption is often the cause. Critical assumptions should be reviewed regularly to check if they are still valid and to determine whether new ones have emerged. When project monitoring reveals that a critical assumption is not holding true or

a risk has materialized, the design of the project or the project's targeted results should be adjusted.

Analyzing and monitoring assumptions and risks serves the additional purpose of helping identify and monitor unintended outcomes and negative effects. Projects may have unintended positive results that were not identified in the DMF. These can be recorded in a monitoring report and the project completion report (PCR). Of greater concern, however, are the unintended negative consequences that projects can have. The possibility that these might occur is classified as a risk. Project teams should monitor for unintended negative consequences of the project and devise an action plan to avoid them or address them if they arise.

E. Link to Strategy 2030 Operational Priorities

The DMF is used to cascade corporate-level indicators to the project level. The corporate results framework contains indicators measuring quantities of outputs and outcomes delivered by completed projects in the seven ADB Strategy 2030 operational priority (OP) areas as well as knowledge products and services. Examples of OP indicators include "people benefiting from increased rural investment," "entities with improved urban planning and financial sustainability," and "cargo transported and energy transmitted across borders." The indicators are cascaded down to the DMF for all operations and TA.

To map to an OP, an operation must meet ADB project classification system eligibility criteria for that OP and contribute results for at least one OP indicator (results framework indicator or tracking indicator). All OP indicators to which the project is expected to contribute results are identified by tagging relevant DMF indicators to relevant OP indicators (Figure 9). A DMF indicator may be tagged to more than one OP indicator and an OP indicator may be tagged to more than one DMF indicator. The number of results the project is expected to achieve for each OP indicator, along with notes on the methodology or data source

---

[7] See ADB. 2018. Project Administration Missions. *Project Administration Instructions.* PAI 6.02. Manila. https://www.adb.org/documents/project-administration-instructions.

Figure 9: Tagging Operational Priority Indicators to Design and Monitoring Framework Indicators

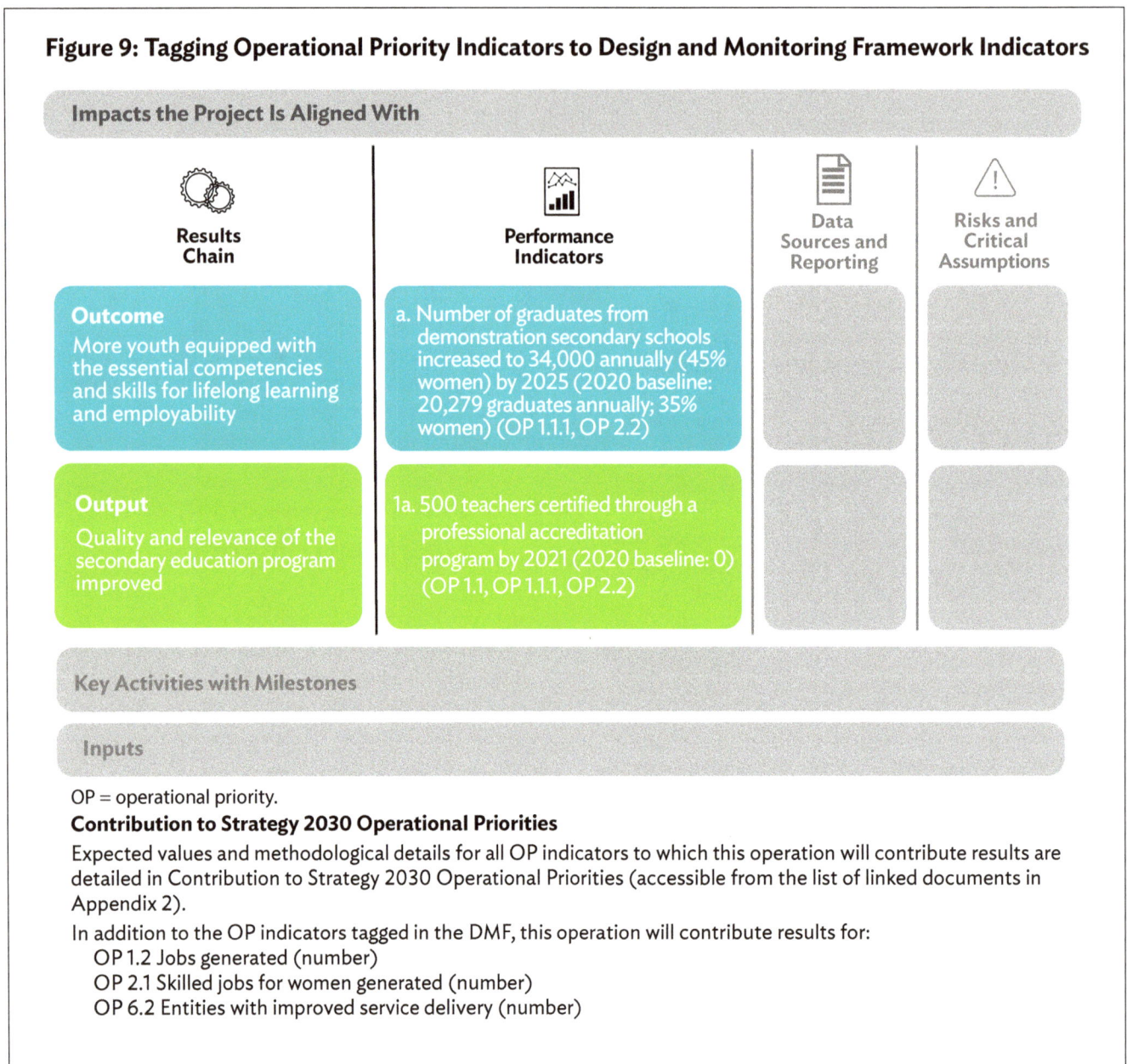

Impacts the Project Is Aligned With

Results Chain	Performance Indicators	Data Sources and Reporting	Risks and Critical Assumptions
Outcome More youth equipped with the essential competencies and skills for lifelong learning and employability	a. Number of graduates from demonstration secondary schools increased to 34,000 annually (45% women) by 2025 (2020 baseline: 20,279 graduates annually; 35% women) (OP 1.1.1, OP 2.2)		
Output Quality and relevance of the secondary education program improved	1a. 500 teachers certified through a professional accreditation program by 2021 (2020 baseline: 0) (OP 1.1, OP 1.1.1, OP 2.2)		

Key Activities with Milestones

Inputs

OP = operational priority.

Contribution to Strategy 2030 Operational Priorities

Expected values and methodological details for all OP indicators to which this operation will contribute results are detailed in Contribution to Strategy 2030 Operational Priorities (accessible from the list of linked documents in Appendix 2).

In addition to the OP indicators tagged in the DMF, this operation will contribute results for:

OP 1.2 Jobs generated (number)
OP 2.1 Skilled jobs for women generated (number)
OP 6.2 Entities with improved service delivery (number)

that will be used to report the number of OP results achieved, are detailed in the RRP linked document, Contribution to Strategy 2030 Operational Priorities. [8]

There are four main scenarios for tagging OP indicators to DMF indicators.

(i) The unit of measure and the target for the OP indicator and DMF indicator are the same. For example, if the DMF indicator is "microfinance loan accounts opened for 5,000 farmers, at least 2,300 women"; the corresponding OP indicator is OP 5.1 "people benefiting from increased rural investment (number). Expected: 5,000; at least 2,300 women." In this case the DMF indicator is tagged to OP 5.1 and the number of results reported for the OP indicator and for the DMF indicator will be the same.

---

[8] For policy-based lending, OP indicators are not tagged in the policy design and monitoring framework (PDMF) as shown in Figure 9. Instead, all OP indicator information is provided exclusively in the RRP linked document Contribution to Strategy 2030 Operational Priorities.

(ii) Several DMF indicators may link to a single OP indicator. For example, the DMF may have multiple indicators measuring people benefiting from various types of improved education and training the project will provide; for example, "number of graduates annually from demonstration secondary schools increased to 34,000, of which at least 45% women"; and "500 teachers certified through a professional accreditation program of which at least 50% women." In this case, both DMF indicators are tagged to OP 1.1. "people benefiting from improved health services, education services, or social protection (number)"; OP 1.1.1 "people enrolled in improved education and/or training (number)"; and OP 2.2 "women and girls completing secondary and tertiary education, and/or other training (number)." The number of results expected for the OP indicators will be the sum of results reported across both DMF indicators (34,500 people; 15,550 women) (Figure 9).

(iii) The DMF indicator and OP indicator may have different units of measure, but the expected value for the OP indicator can be calculated by converting the DMF target into the OP indicator's unit of measurement. For example, the DMF indicator could be "households in City B receiving 24-hour potable water supply increased to 500,000." This DMF indicator is tagged to OP 4.1 "people benefiting from improved services in urban areas (number)." The conversion method used to determine the expected value for the OP indicator is explained in the RRP linked document. In the above example, data on the average number of people per household in City B should be used to determine the number of people benefiting.

(iv) The OP indicator may be a proxy or leading indicator for the DMF indicator, or vice versa, or it may otherwise be indirectly measured by the

DMF indicator. For example, the DMF indicator "at least 100 management staff received merit-based certificates from completing TVET leadership training, of which 10% female" is a leading indicator for OP 2.3.1 "women with strengthened leadership capacities (number)" for which the expected OP value will be 10 women. It is expected that the knowledge and skills women gain in TVET leadership will contribute to their overall leadership capacity.

The DMF template provides the option to list OP indicators below the DMF table instead of tagging them within it. This option is used in cases where a project is expected to contribute results for an OP indicator, but there is no clear link to one or more DMF indicators. Cases where this exception may occur include when (i) results for the OP indicator will be achieved through all or nearly all project outputs; for example, all project outputs will contribute results for OP2.1 jobs generated (number); or (ii) when the OP results are not considered appropriate to include as targets in the project DMF; for example, an urban rail transit project may contribute results for OP 3.1 total annual greenhouse gas emissions reduction (tons of carbon dioxide equivalent/year) but this result is a positive externality expected from the project and not an outcome target. In these cases, OP indicators are noted below the DMF table (Figure 9) and the expected value to be delivered, data collection methodology, and data source are detailed in the RRP linked document, Contribution to Strategy 2030 Priorities.

For each project, OP indicators and their expected values are entered into e-Operations and tracked, and results achieved are reported by project completion. As with DMF indicators, any changes in the quantity of results expected to be delivered for OP indicators should be revised during project implementation and reflected in e-Operations.

III. Design and Monitoring Framework Formulation Process

The process used to design a project, including its DMF, is critical to the eventual success of the project. Projects define an agreement between borrowers, intended beneficiaries, and ADB on expected project results and causal links between result levels, risks and critical assumptions, and the indicators and targets that will be used to measure performance. The DMF articulates and communicates the planned performance of the project. Its quality relies on a good design process to ensure that the planned results are achievable and will meet the needs of the intended beneficiaries.

Ideally, all stakeholders (intended beneficiaries and other parties) should be involved in a participatory process to determine the range of existing problems and decide which of them the project should address. The stakeholders should also be involved in determining the solutions the project will deliver and the targets the project should achieve. This may include applying approaches such as human-centered design, which involve intended beneficiaries extensively in the design and testing of potential solutions. Regardless of the approach used, a project that is designed in isolation from its intended beneficiaries is less likely to succeed.

While the extent of stakeholder participation will vary by project, it is equally important in every project (Box 12). Even projects that have disparate and dispersed beneficiaries, such as those that reform national systems or processes, or large infrastructure projects such as a highway, wind farm, or a container port, benefit from stakeholder participation. The nature of these projects makes beneficiary consultation more challenging. However, the siting, construction, and operation of infrastructure often affect local populations and therefore, at the very least, the projects benefit from stakeholder consultation to reduce localized negative effects. In addition, design modifications can ensure some benefits accrue to poor or marginalized groups, thus making the project more inclusive.

> **Box 12: Three Reasons Why a Participatory Approach Is Important**
>
> (i) Projects must be designed to respond to the needs of intended beneficiaries (people or organizations) in relevant and appropriate ways. Intended beneficiaries are the most knowledgeable about the problems they face and how their needs can be met. Projects cannot be properly designed to address problems and provide solutions to meet needs without involving the intended beneficiaries and other key stakeholders.
>
> (ii) Project stakeholders will be more committed to implementing a design they helped create.
>
> (iii) A group process usually produces a higher-quality, more relevant design and monitoring framework, as groups can make better decisions than any one individual. The participatory process could involve the borrower, executing and implementing agencies, other government organizations, civil society organizations, the private sector, intended beneficiaries, and the Asian Development Bank project team and consultants.

A project should ideally be conceived through the following five main steps. Steps (i) to (iii) comprise the situation analysis, while steps (iv) and (v) correspond to solution development (Figure 10).

(i) **Align with country priorities.** Select a key outcome from the country partnership strategy results framework in the country operations business plan (COBP).[9]

(ii) **Conduct stakeholder analysis.** Identify and define the role of stakeholders who can significantly influence or are important in a particular context, for example, a development problem, issue, or sector.

---

[9] For TA projects, this step may not apply.

Figure 10: The Process to Produce a Design and Monitoring Framework

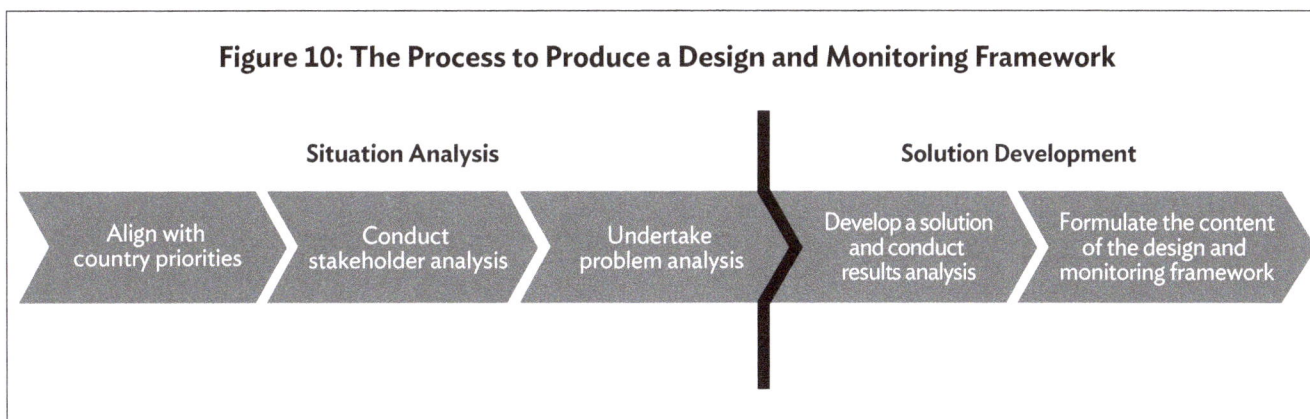

Situation Analysis   **Solution Development**

Align with country priorities → Conduct stakeholder analysis → Undertake problem analysis → Develop a solution and conduct results analysis → Formulate the content of the design and monitoring framework

(iii) **Undertake problem analysis.** Identify the development problem(s) to be addressed. In consultation with key stakeholders, identify and analyze the nature and underlying causes of the problem(s) and their effects (Box 13). Develop a problem analysis diagram to help conduct a thorough problem analysis and visually communicate it. This diagram is required for all sovereign operations and is optional for TA.

(iv) **Develop a solution and conduct results analysis.** Identify improvements that may be made within a given time frame and determine the scope of the proposed project, ensuring the design is based on a well-researched theory of change (ToC). A ToC diagram can also be drawn to aid a thorough results analysis and visually communicate it.

(v) **Formulate the content of the design and monitoring framework.** Decide on the DMF results chain and complete the DMF template.

This general process is relevant even in cases where the developing member country (DMC) approaches ADB to finance a project they have already identified. In these cases, steps (i) to (v) should still be taken to validate the project concept and inform the detailed design. Tips for applying good project design practices within different operational realities are provided throughout this section.

Box 13: Tips for Resourcing a Participatory Design Process

Asian Development Bank project teams can draw on several sources of financing to support thorough and participatory situation analysis and solution development for a project. Approved along with the project concept paper, transaction technical assistance funds can finance consultants who can support further stakeholder consultation, for example conduct surveys or facilitate consultation workshops, to further expand and validate the initial problem analysis conducted for the concept paper and help develop a high-quality design and monitoring framework. Project readiness financing, knowledge and support technical assistance, and some Asian Development Bank-administered trust funds can also finance these activities even before the project concept paper is approved.

A. Align with Country Priorities

For sovereign operations, the starting point of the analysis is the country partnership strategy results framework in the COBP and related summary sector or thematic assessments. This results framework contains key outcomes that ADB projects will support.[10] The outcome specified in the DMF should

DMF Formulation Process

---

[10] For more details, see ADB. Forthcoming. *Guidelines for Country Partnership Strategy Results Frameworks.* Manila. https://www.adb.org/documents/preparing-results-frameworks-and-monitoring-results-country-and-sector-levels.

be aligned with at least one of these key outcomes. However, depending on the project results, the alignment may be closer at the national development impact level. Disaster response projects are exempted from this step. For TA projects, the link may be to the summary sector or thematic assessment, a regional strategy, or another high-level strategy or plan.

B. Conduct Stakeholder Analysis

Planning is more effective when it is done with the participation of key stakeholders. It is therefore important to conduct stakeholder analysis when preparing any project. The ultimate goal when conducting stakeholder analysis is to assess the needs of affected citizens. The analysis is done during the due diligence phase, and it is good practice to review, reassess, and possibly repeat it at strategic intervals throughout the project cycle.

All projects involve several key stakeholders. In general, stakeholders may be categorized as government, civil society (including citizens and CSOs), and the private sector. Stakeholders are the agencies, organizations, groups, or individuals that have a direct or indirect interest in the project and the development problems it seeks to address. Stakeholders may affect, be affected by, or perceive to be affected by a decision, activity, or result of the project. Key stakeholders of ADB-financed projects vary depending on the nature of the project. Common ones include the borrower; the executing agency; the implementing agency; other government agencies at central and local levels; civil society, including nongovernment organizations and advocacy groups; private sector representatives; citizens at large, including intended beneficiaries, marginalized groups, and those potentially negatively affected; and development partners.

Stakeholder analysis is a diagnostic process that enables the project team, working closely with project stakeholders, to identify key stakeholders, including intermediaries and intended beneficiaries, their relationships to each other, and their level of interest in, and influence over, the issues at hand. It helps understand the interests of important and influential stakeholders in relation to the development problems, project results, and potential safeguard issues. It also helps identify which groups are supportive and which may oppose the project strategy and subsequently obstruct project implementation, and provides a sound basis for taking appropriate actions to gain the support of opponents and to get key supporters more involved. The findings of stakeholder analysis are the basis for the problem analysis and are used to inform project identification, design (including developing tailored behavior change communication approaches as relevant), and implementation.

Process. Stakeholder analysis includes the following steps.[11]

(i) Based on the issue(s) the project will address, consider the potential geographic areas and beneficiaries that the project could assist. The project could consider, for example, the issues of transport in rural areas, elderly care, or urban air quality. Identify all the stakeholders involved in the issue(s), grouping them by category (e.g., intended beneficiary groups, public sector organizations, CSOs, advocacy groups, private companies, and development partner agencies). Be sure to distinguish among the different subsections of the stakeholder group as relevant to the context. Specifically, it is important to identify marginalized groups and subgroups; for example, an elderly population may need to be differentiated by socioeconomic status, ethnicity, and/or gender.

(ii) Determine the interests of each group with reference to each issue (e.g., elderly care, youth skills development, disabled inclusion). Record how and why they are involved, the level of intensity of their interests and concerns, their expectations, and their potential to benefit or suffer as a result of any changes to the context or situation surrounding the issue.

---

[11] For detailed guidance and tools for effectively engaging stakeholders throughout the project cycle, consult ADB. 2012. *Strengthening Participation for Development Results: An Asian Development Bank Guide to Participation.* Manila. https://www.adb.org/sites/default/files/institutional-document/33349/files/strengthening-participation-development-results.pdf.

(iii) Determine which problems each group perceives are surrounding each issue (e.g., What are the problems associated with elderly care?). Record clear problem statements that describe the effects on those affected (e.g., for the issue of transport in rural areas, the problem should be stated as "travel is long, uncomfortable, and expensive" [correct]; rather than "no road maintenance system" [incorrect]).

(iv) Identify the resources—financial and nonfinancial—each group has put, or could raise, toward each issue. This includes resources to support or prevent change. Formal organizations have both financial and nonfinancial resources, while population and civil society groups have predominantly nonfinancial resources. These can include labor, political influence, votes, readiness to strike, and public pressure.

(v) List the mandates or formal authority that stakeholders must carry out in a particular function, as appropriate. Generally, population groups, such as low-income groups, farmers, and women, do not have mandates.

There are various tools to support project teams in conducting this process, including a simple stakeholder analysis table (Figure 11), which is useful for compiling and communicating the information for each step.

Steps (ii)–(v) are best done using a participatory process. Suitable approaches range from basic consultations and focus group discussions to more hands-on brainstorming sessions and workshops. The project team should use their judgment to determine which is most appropriate, bearing in mind the main objective is to identify all key stakeholders, accurately capture their interests and perspectives, and help secure their buy-in. Practical factors to consider include the cost of workshops and alternative means of communication, support to ensure the inclusion of women, availability of local licensed group facilitators or moderators, and time constraints. At a minimum, the process should include representatives of different stakeholder groups identified by the borrower, project team, and resident mission.

To reach out to beneficiaries and communities effectively, ADB typically works with CSOs to organize workshops and consultations. The CSOs' familiarity with local communities and their expertise in participatory approaches make them suitable organizers of community-based consultations. Representatives of marginalized groups bring experience and specialized participatory skills that are valuable for ensuring effective inclusion, particularly of marginalized groups (e.g., women facilitators and youth in peer-to-peer focus group discussions). Workshops should be led by an experienced facilitator. The workshops can include mixed groups of stakeholders or representatives of a single group. If there are power dynamics that may prevent certain groups from expressing their views, then it is best to hold workshops with these groups separately, at least initially (Box 14).

There is a tendency, especially in the case of large projects with disparate and dispersed beneficiaries, for planning teams not to involve certain stakeholders in the planning process. It is important to ensure consultations follow the principles of consensus-building and conflict resolution, and that representatives consulted adequately represent the various interest groups. Make sure to include the following groups.

Figure 11: Stakeholder Analysis Table Template

Stakeholder (i)	Stakeholder's Interest (ii)	Perceived Problems (iii)	Resources (iv)	Mandate (v)

Box 14: Tips for Conducting Participatory Stakeholder Consultations

(i) Select stakeholders that adequately represent relevant groups and sectors.

(ii) Ensure participants are informed about the topics and issues for discussion in advance of the consultation. Provide briefing materials as early as possible and in a language the stakeholders understand.

(iii) Manage expectations and clarify upfront with participants which areas are to be covered by the consultation.

(iv) After the consultation, give stakeholders feedback about how their comments have been considered.

(v) Although civil society organizations are the usual intermediaries for reaching citizens, it may also be possible to consult citizens through other means such as social media or other forms of technology.

• **Marginalized groups.** These groups are often left out on the assumption that they are not well enough informed or educated to be able to contribute. Leaving out these groups, who are often main intended beneficiaries of projects, is a costly mistake. Consequences include a less relevant project design and implementation challenges later on. Remember the motto, "nothing about us without us" and avoid missing key stakeholders by asking, "Whose voice is not normally heard on this issue?" Project teams should take proactive steps to engage women's organizations, both formal and informal, and to involve women from marginalized groups during consultations and focus group discussions.

• **Groups with negative or opposing views.** Groups who might have negative or opposing views on the development issue or project strategy have the potential to obstruct the project. Involving them in project design is important to ensure their concerns are heard

and considered early on and to increase the likelihood that they will accept and subsequently support the project.

• **Groups essential to project sustainability.** Include stakeholders who may not be involved in project implementation but who will be involved after the project has been completed, such as agencies or groups that will operate and maintain project outputs. Involving these stakeholders in the design is critical for ensuring the sustainability of the project's results.

Stakeholder analysis and engagement should continue throughout the project cycle because it fulfills different functions at different stages. During problem identification, it serves to identify important and influential stakeholders and draws attention to how to involve them in the analytical and planning process. During project formulation, it guides design decisions and the analysis of assumptions and risks. During project implementation, it helps develop strategies to keep stakeholders informed, track their changing circumstances and interests, and plan their possible involvement during implementation.

C.   Undertake Problem Analysis

Problem analysis is the second diagnostic process in situation analysis. A thorough problem analysis provides an understanding of the main problems and binding constraints (e.g., economic, cultural, sociopolitical, environmental, and gender equality related) surrounding the issue or issues the project will address; and the causes of the main problems and their effects on the lives of people (including women and men of all ages, ability, socioeconomic status, and ethnicity); communities; and organizations. Once completed, a good problem analysis informs a relevant project design and provides a clear rationale for why it is important to invest in the project.

ADB uses the problem analysis diagram as a tool to support thorough problem analysis and communicate it visually to key stakeholders. This tool is used to (i) analyze the existing situation surrounding an issue or set of issues, (ii) identify the major problems and constraints, and (iii) visualize the cause-and-effect relationship diagrammatically. The concept paper for a sovereign project includes a problem analysis diagram; for TA it is optional.

There are two main approaches teams can use for the diagram.

(i)   The diagram can present an in-depth analysis of the major problems and associated constraints related to the issue the proposed project will focus on (e.g., "technical and vocational education in province A," or "livability of city B"). This type of problem analysis diagram is prepared during concept paper preparation and the associated reconnaissance mission, and it can be further developed during RRP preparation and associated fact-finding missions.

(ii) Alternatively, the diagram can present a broader analysis of the major problems and associated constraints affecting one or more issue areas or sectors in the DMC or group of DMCs (e.g., "plastic pollution in the oceans of region X," "livability of cities in DMC X," "public financial management in DMC X," or "energy sector in DMC X"). This broader type of problem analysis diagram may have been prepared as part of the country sector or thematic assessment.

Various designs can be used to develop a problem analysis diagram. Figure 12 provides an illustrative example. A good diagram brings clarity to a complex context by illustrating the main problems and the cause-and-effect relationships between them. This may include illustrating problems that are mutually reinforcing (i.e., interconnected in a "vicious cycle") by using a double-headed arrow, and using horizontal and vertical arrows to illustrate causal connections between various problems. There is no minimum or limit to the number of boxes in a diagram. Project teams can decide on the appropriate scope and depth of analysis. Too narrow a scope is of limited analytical value and may oversimplify the issue, leading to an inadequate solution analysis. On the other hand, it is important to keep focused on the main issue area because too broad a focus will cause a loss of direction and clarity among stakeholders.

Process. Problem analysis should be undertaken in a participatory manner, in consultation with key stakeholders identified during the stakeholder analysis (Box 15). Furthermore, stakeholder analysis should continue during the problem analysis stage. When conducting a problem analysis, key questions to ask for each issue explored are: "Who does this affect most?" "Who controls or manages this?" "Who decides or is formally responsible for this?" "Who has the power to change this?" The ADB team is responsible for finding a suitable way to involve the stakeholders effectively, considering the local context. Ideally, the problem analysis diagram is developed during a half- or full-day workshop with key stakeholders, or a series of smaller stakeholder workshops from which the results are merged into a comprehensive diagram.

A good problem analysis incorporates data and information from different sources. Start with any research and data that already exist, including studies and analyses of the issue, and documentation from previous projects addressing the same or a similar issue, especially evaluation studies. Refer also to key strategic frameworks such as the ADB country partnership strategy, national development strategies and plans, and national and subnational sector strategies and plans. Complement and validate this document-based information with information collected directly from key stakeholders and subject-matter experts via interviews, meetings, and/or focus groups, and from site observations by the project team.

> **Box 15: Tips for Applying Good Practices to Suit Operational Realities: Situation Analysis**
>
> Sometimes developing member countries approach the Asian Development Bank to finance a project they have already identified and may also have already designed to some degree. In these cases, the Asian Development Bank project team should confirm the extent to which the proposed project has been informed by a participatory and evidence-based situation analysis. It is useful to review the stakeholder and problem analyses with key stakeholders to ensure the proposed project and its design are relevant.

Figure 12: Problem Analysis Diagram Example for a Livable City Project Focused on Transport Systems

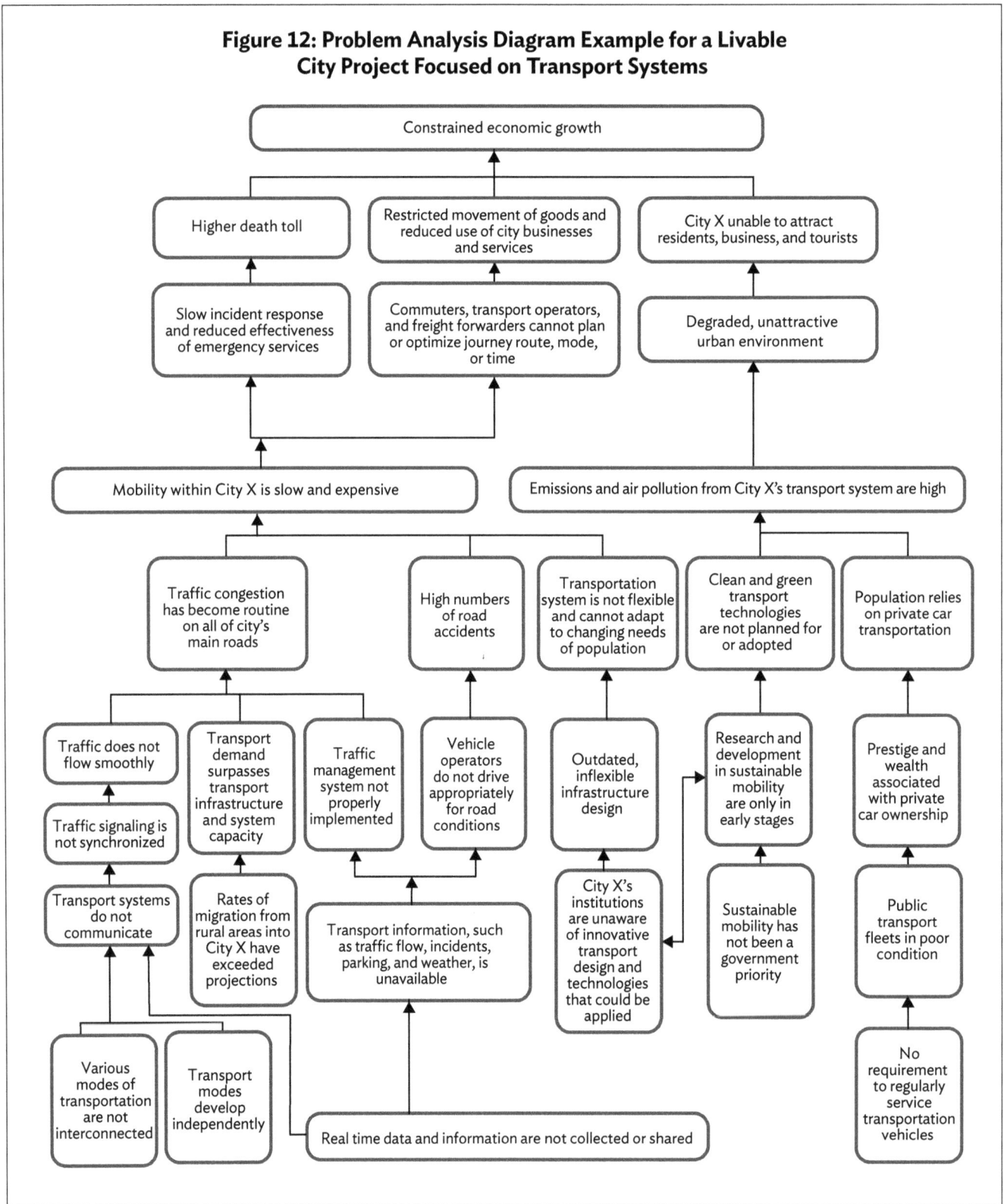

Constrained economic growth

Higher death toll

Restricted movement of goods and reduced use of city businesses and services

City X unable to attract residents, business, and tourists

Slow incident response and reduced effectiveness of emergency services

Commuters, transport operators, and freight forwarders cannot plan or optimize journey route, mode, or time

Degraded, unattractive urban environment

Mobility within City X is slow and expensive

Emissions and air pollution from City X's transport system are high

Traffic congestion has become routine on all of city's main roads

High numbers of road accidents

Transportation system is not flexible and cannot adapt to changing needs of population

Clean and green transport technologies are not planned for or adopted

Population relies on private car transportation

Traffic does not flow smoothly

Transport demand surpasses transport infrastructure and system capacity

Traffic management system not properly implemented

Vehicle operators do not drive appropriately for road conditions

Outdated, inflexible infrastructure design

Research and development in sustainable mobility are only in early stages

Prestige and wealth associated with private car ownership

Traffic signaling is not synchronized

Transport systems do not communicate

Rates of migration from rural areas into City X have exceeded projections

Transport information, such as traffic flow, incidents, parking, and weather, is unavailable

City X's institutions are unaware of innovative transport design and technologies that could be applied

Sustainable mobility has not been a government priority

Public transport fleets in poor condition

Various modes of transportation are not interconnected

Transport modes develop independently

Real time data and information are not collected or shared

No requirement to regularly service transportation vehicles

A problem analysis diagram can be developed through four main steps.

(i) **Identify an initial set of problems surrounding the issue.** Brainstorm a few problems related to the issue, drawing on documented data and information and inputs from key stakeholders. When stating a problem, ensure the following:

  (a) State the problem as a negative condition or reality, not in terms of specific things being unavailable or the solution being absent. For example, stating a problem as "lack of technical and vocational education and training (TVET) institutes in rural areas" formulates the problem in terms of what is missing and may lead to a project being created to build TVET institutes; whereas "a high proportion of rural unemployed youth are not enrolled in educational programs" states a factual problem that could have several underlying causes, including cultural, economic, or other factors such as low level of interest in existing TVET programs among youth. This latter problem statement facilitates a more thorough analysis that can help the team consider a broader range of more relevant solutions.

  (b) Be specific and clear. For example, "rural road maintenance by district road authorities does not meet national quality standards" is better than "poor quality of maintenance."

  (c) Ensure ownership by a stakeholder or group. Problem identification focuses on what is happening and to whom. This should involve discussions about whether particular groups are affected more than others. A good problem statement is described from the perspective of those it affects. For example, "travel in rural areas of the district is time consuming, uncomfortable, and expensive" is better than "suboptimal rural transit"; and "subnational government institutions lack expertise in budget management" is better than "lack of institutional

capacity." A helpful guiding question is "are we adequately capturing the specific problems facing institutions and key groups, especially men and women, minorities, and marginalized groups?"

(ii) **Identify direct causes.** Identify the major causes of each problem by asking "what causes this to happen?" It is often helpful to think in terms of categories of causes, such as policy constraints, institutional constraints, capacity weaknesses, or social or cultural norms. Repeat step (ii) viewing direct causes as problems and asking, "why has this happened?" Place the direct causes of each of these problems below. Continue to drill down until the analysis is exhausted and specific root causes are identified. The number of problems shown in the diagram is not restricted and will vary based on the nature and complexity of the issue being analyzed. Figure 13 illustrates the question-and-answer logic used to build the diagram.

(iii) **Identify direct effects.** Starting from the problems at the top of the problem analysis diagram, identify the direct effects by asking the question, "What are the effects of this problem?" for each problem statement. Formulate the answer as a problem statement and place it above the problem statement it is linked to. Continue to specify effects until the final effects are reached.

(iv) **Review and refine.** Refine the problem analysis diagram by reviewing the interrelationships between each problem statement. To check the logic, ask the question, "Why does this occur?"

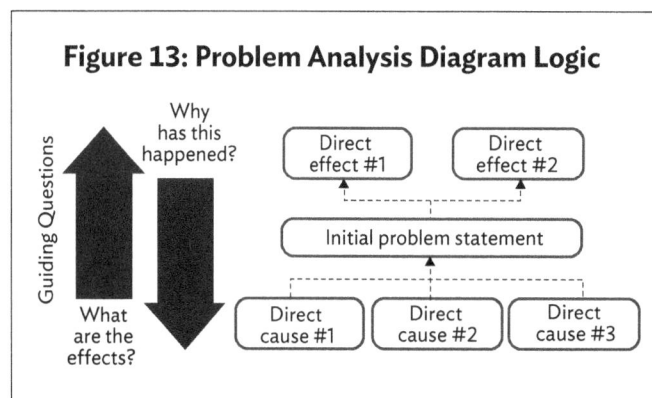

Figure 13: Problem Analysis Diagram Logic

as you move downward from one problem statement to the next. The response should provide a clear direct cause; if there is a major leap in logic, fill in the gap with one or more additional problem statements. It is unlikely that the first formulation of the problem analysis diagram will be correct. Problem statements and cause-and-effect links may need factual verification through research or further consultation with stakeholders or technical experts. Different stakeholders may also need to be consulted as new issues are uncovered during the analysis.

D.   Solution Development and Results Analysis

The findings of a thorough situation analysis are the foundation from which the project team can develop the right solutions to achieve the desired development results. Moving from situation analysis to solution development involves identifying and analyzing desired results and scoping a package of effective solutions that is realistically implementable given the resources available. Like problem analysis, these steps should be undertaken in a participatory manner, in consultation with key stakeholders identified during the stakeholder analysis. The theory of change (ToC) is a useful analytical approach for undertaking solution development and results analysis, which are two iterative processes that inform each other.

Theory of change approach. Every project design has an underlying ToC, which is essentially a set of expectations held by the project team about how the project will bring about positive change for its intended beneficiaries. A good project design is based on a well-researched (i.e., evidence-based) ToC developed in consultation with, and agreed upon by, key stakeholders. Applying the ToC approach involves making the ToC explicit and using it as a tool to help develop and communicate a fitting project design, and support project management and evaluation.

Making the ToC explicit involves specifying the project's development hypothesis by mapping the pathways of change between the results the project aims to achieve (outputs and outcome), how the project plans to achieve them (activities) and the assumptions and risks underlying these change pathways. Although the results chain as depicted in the DMF shows a linear logical chain leading to the outcome, the cause-and-effect relationships are rarely simple and linear. Mapping out the ToC helps the project design team comprehensively think through the complexity of the change process and can stimulate innovative project designs. The ToC is best mapped and communicated with a diagram and accompanying narrative. Figure 14 provides an illustrative example of a ToC diagram template.

Applying the theory of change approach to ADB projects. At the very least, the project description narrative in the RRP should outline the basic ToC of the project by explaining the essential cause-and-effect relationships between the project's outputs and outcome, identifying critical assumptions and risks, and justifying these and other project design choices with evidence from robust economic, and poverty and social analyses;[12] evidence and lessons from other comparable interventions (including by other development partners, government, and civil society); and evaluations or other research.

Project teams may also decide to prepare a more comprehensive ToC analysis and visualize it in a ToC diagram (Box 16). While the ToC can be described in narrative form, visualizing it in a flowchart yields

---

[12]   A project's results logic should be founded on robust economic, and poverty and social analyses, from which the summary findings are included as linked documents to the RRP. The economic analysis tests and establishes the economic rationale and viability of the proposed design, including an analysis of alternative designs or projects. The poverty and social analysis assesses the key poverty and social issues of the potential beneficiaries, including the project's impact channels and expected systemic changes. Refer to ADB. 2017. *Guidelines for the Economic Analysis of Projects.* Manila. https://www.adb.org/sites/default/files/institutional-document/32256/economic-analysis-projects.pdf; and ADB. 2012. *Handbook on Poverty and Social Analysis: A Working Document.* Manila. https://www.adb.org/sites/default/files/institutional-document/33763/files/handbook-poverty-social-analysis.pdf.

Figure 14: Example Theory of Change Diagram Template

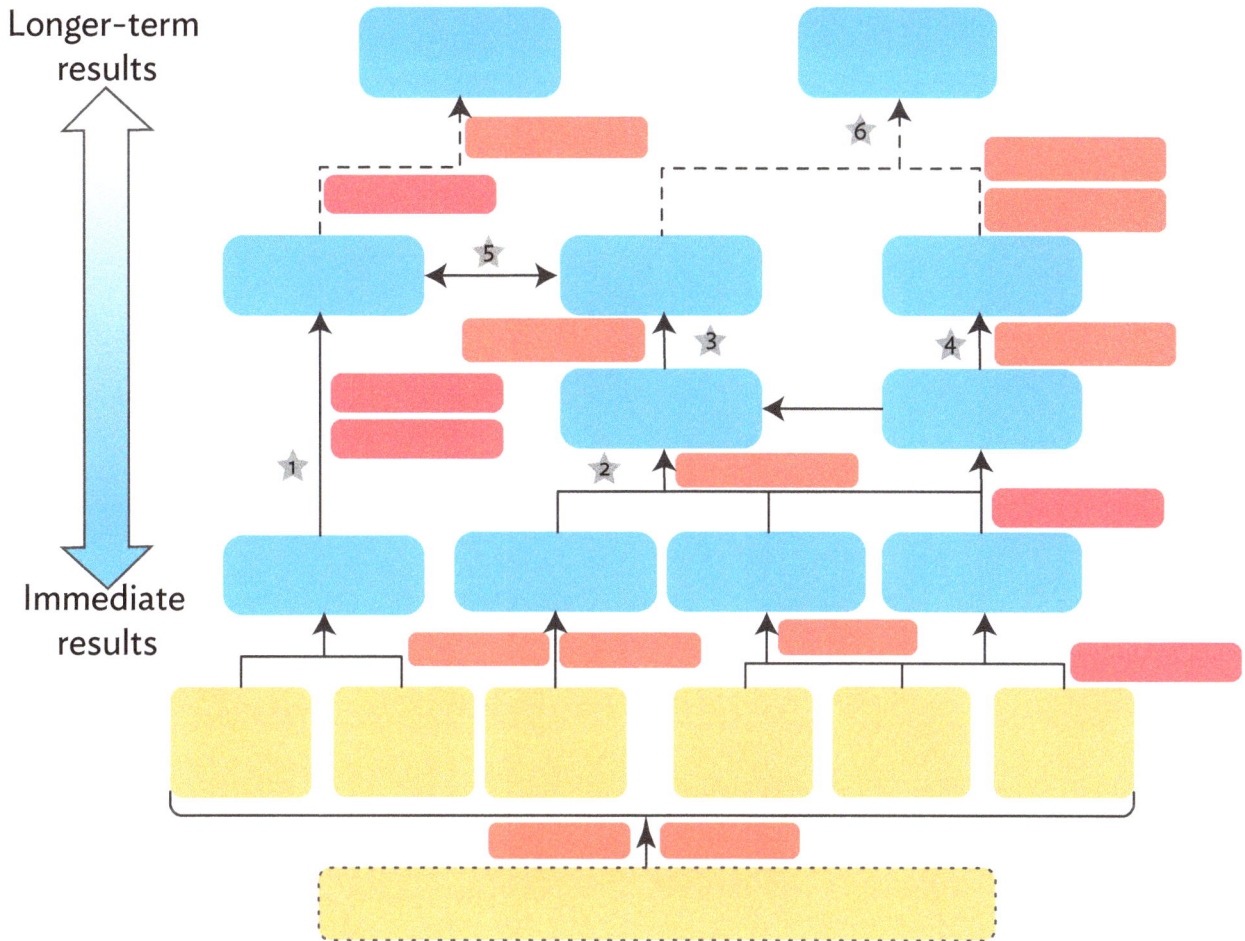

Longer-term results

Immediate results

Evidence:
1
2
3
4
5
6

Legend:
- Results
- Activities
- Inputs
- Assumption
- Risk
- Reference to evidence
- Contribution
- Direct causal pathway

Box 16: Tips for Visualizing and Communicating the Theory of Change

(i) The theory of change (ToC) can be mapped in differing forms and formats and contain varying depths of information and detail. The vertical flowchart diagram design depicted in Figure 14 is recommended as it mirrors the vertical logic of the design and monitoring framework.

(ii) No matter what style is selected, a good ToC mapping should be logical, show detailed coherent cause-and-effect pathways, and clearly communicate how the project design is expected to achieve the intended results.

(iii) It is challenging to capture all the key details in a ToC diagram. Include a supporting narrative that explains the details and includes the evidence basis underpinning the cause-and-effect pathways.

a helpful analytical and communication tool. A flowchart is especially useful for complex, multi-issue or multisector project designs because it helps the design team identify and comprehensively think through the multifaceted change pathways. It is also an effective visual means for communicating the ToC to key project stakeholders, including reviewers and project managers.

When DMCs approach ADB to finance a project that they have already identified, and may also have designed to some degree, it can still be useful to map out the ToC to ensure the design is relevant and comprehensive enough to sustainably solve the targeted development problems, and to confirm the design with key stakeholders. In cases where ADB replicates a common or previously implemented project design in a new location, mapping out the ToC can help ensure the design suits the contextual particularities of the new location.

Process. Mapping the ToC is an iterative process. Start with a simple version and build it out over the

course of project preparation. Mapping the ToC collaboratively with key stakeholders helps develop effective solutions and a shared understanding among stakeholders of what the project will try to accomplish and how. It is also useful to build consensus on how success will be measured and documented. While the process is ideally undertaken collaboratively with key stakeholders in a series of workshops, alternative approaches can be adopted to suit the operational realities of different project contexts (Box 17).

Box 17: Tips for Applying Good Practices to Suit Operational Realities: Mapping the Theory of Change

There is no substitute for a highly participatory approach to mapping the theory of change (ToC), but it is not always feasible. Operational realities sometimes require alternative approaches to be taken. Common challenges include tight project preparation timelines and the impracticality of gathering all key stakeholders. In these cases, the following alternative approaches can be taken (in order from more to less ideal):

(i) The Asian Development Bank (ADB) project team drafts the ToC and performance indicators via a participatory in-person or virtual workshop with key stakeholders. The ADB team subsequently finalizes the ToC and prepares a draft design and monitoring framework (DMF), which it then shares with key project stakeholders for feedback and input.

(ii) The ADB project team drafts the ToC and performance indicators for the project and shares and finalizes them with key stakeholders via participatory workshops.

(iii) The ADB project team drafts the ToC and DMF for the project and shares it electronically with key project stakeholders for feedback and input.

In cases where a project DMF has already been developed, mapping the ToC underlying it can still be a helpful tool for validating the project results chain and design, and identifying any needed adjustments. Regardless of the approach taken, it is essential to allocate time with key stakeholders to review and discuss the ToC and DMF at the project launch.

Suggested steps for undertaking solution development and results analysis using the ToC approach are as follows:

(i) **Identify starter result(s).** Considering the findings from the problem analysis, convert the problem statements into results statements—positive statements that describe the situation after the problems have been resolved, or the change we want to achieve. For example: "youth perceive secondary school as irrelevant" may become "secondary school curriculum is engaging and relevant to labor market demands."

- Ensure results statements are (a) phrased as specifically as possible, including identifying who or what should have changed, and in what way, and specifying the intended beneficiaries; and (b) ambitious yet realistic for a project to deliver. For example, the problem statement "cost of transporting goods to market is prohibitive for farmers" may become a results statement such as "cost of transporting goods to market is more affordable for farmers," not "transport of goods to market is free of cost."
- The problem analysis diagram can be converted into a skeleton of the ToC simply by converting all problem statements into results statements.

(ii) **Map the pathways of change.** Starting from the highest-level results statements, work backward step-by-step to identify what needs to change before the situation described in the level above can be achieved or occur. This process is called "backward mapping" because it involves starting at the higher-level results and working backward to the beginning by repeatedly asking, "What are the necessary preconditions for the above change to occur?" Figure 15 illustrates the question-and-answer logic used to build out the diagram. Review and refine the cause-and-effect pathways ensuring there are no leaps in logic between statements.

- In each results statement, make sure to name the stakeholders involved and their changed behavior, performance, or situation. At each

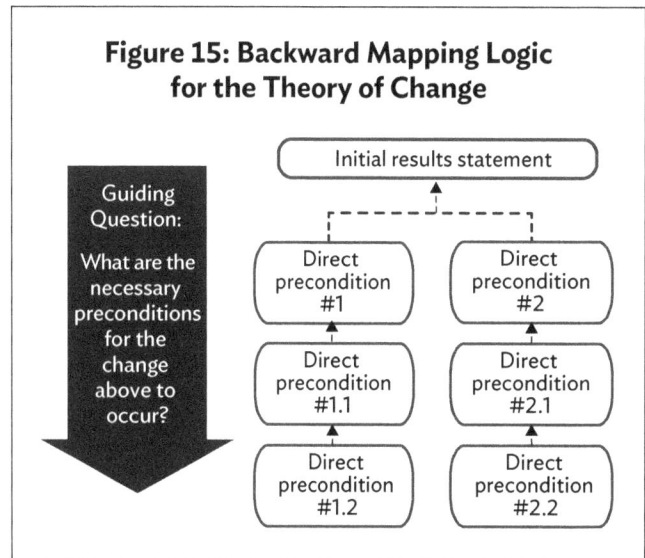

Figure 15: Backward Mapping Logic for the Theory of Change

level, answer and specify: "Who is doing what differently?" and "What is there that was not there before?"

- Tip: Often, project design teams are inclined to focus on what they or the project must do to create the desired change. This trap of jumping to project activities should be avoided because it prematurely narrows creativity in project design down to the familiar menu of activities. There is a simple way to help avoid the activities-focused trap: the results statements must be change statements. They should not say anything about what the project is doing. For example, avoid a statement like "train staff in organization X"; instead use "staff of organization X have improved knowledge of Y topic." This approach spurs innovation by encouraging teams to brainstorm various strategies for bringing about the desired changes.

Box 18 provides some tips on tools and applications that can be used to map a ToC.

(iii) **Identify change pathway owners and explore solutions and project design strategies.** Develop appropriate solutions that can achieve the desired results.

Box 18: Tips on Tools for Mapping the Theory of Change

Various tools and applications can be used to build a theory of change diagram in a participatory manner. A common approach is to convene the key stakeholders (physically or virtually) and use sticky notes to brainstorm. Sticky notes can be moved and reordered making this a helpful and accessible way to engage participants. In this approach, participants work together to draft results statements (one per sticky note) and then organize them in a flowchart. Various software and web-based applications, such as Microsoft PowerPoint and Draw.io, support a versatile mock-up of flowcharts and virtual team cocreation.

- Identify which stakeholders have the most influence on, and vested interest in, achieving changes in each pathway of change. They may be (a) the holders of the official mandate for improving undesirable conditions, (b) stakeholder groups that need to coordinate their regular tasks and resources to achieve a change, or (c) individuals who wield official or unofficial power to champion or lead a change process. This information will be available from a good stakeholder analysis.
- Identify project design strategies (sets of outputs and activities) that can bring about or influence the desired changes. Based on the list of options, consult with the main owners of the change pathways to identify outputs and activities that are the most relevant, promising, and feasible.
- If not already mapped, add these outputs and activities to the ToC diagram.

(iv) **Articulate assumptions and risks.** Note the assumptions and risks inherent in your pathways of change, especially with respect to the following.
- The causal relationship between activities and outputs, and levels of results in the pathway. Ask: "If X changes, will Z really happen? Why? Under which conditions would this work? What might derail this? Is there anything we are taking for granted?"
- The response of stakeholders to specific project activities and outputs and the changes that are expected as a result. Ask: "Are our assumptions about causality valid for all stakeholder groups and subgroups (e.g., women and men, the poor and marginalized)? Will some stakeholder groups respond or behave differently than others?"
- (Pre)conditions in the project context that need to be in place for the desired change to occur. Ask: "What evidence do we have that supports our assumptions about causality and the effectiveness of the selected project design?" "What risks could derail our plan?"
- See Section II.D for further guidance on identifying and analyzing assumptions and risks and the decision tree for identifying critical assumptions in Figure 7.

The analysis of assumptions and risks may reveal that adjustments to the change pathways are required, and/or that additional outputs or activities will be needed to bring about the desired changes for all intended beneficiaries.

(v) **Consider unintended effects and sustainability.** Review the ToC asking the following questions.
- "Are there any unintended consequences—positive or negative—that may occur as a consequence of planned activities or the achievement of intended results?" Note these and adjust project design and/or identify risks to be mitigated, as necessary.
- "Will the intended results be sustained beyond project completion?" "Which beneficiaries' needs will continue during the post-completion phase?" Adjust project design as necessary to include the inputs and activities required to sustain the results. Identify the risks to achieving sustainability readiness and possible mitigating measures.

(vi) **Confirm project scope.** A fully developed ToC diagram will contain a series of results chains (outputs and outcomes). Confirm which results chains the project will deliver. Each stakeholder group, the executing agency, and the project team need to clearly understand how moving forward with a particular results chain will affect them directly or indirectly.

- During this analysis, consider the available resources, capacities of the executing and implementing agencies, interests of the intended beneficiaries, political feasibility, and other variables affecting successful implementation of the results chain. If a results chain owner is unable to commit to its achievement, consider whether the strategy for achieving the results chain should be improved so the results chain owner stands a better chance of success. Solutions may come from expert knowledge, best practices, and lessons from other projects or programs. If the results chain owner accepts this new strategy, then include this results chain branch in the project's scope. If the results chain owner cannot accept the strategy, then these results chains will have to be excluded from the project.

- Identify which clusters of outputs will be delivered by the ADB-financed project. In so doing, confirm their suitability given ADB project selection criteria. These may be economic, financial, socioeconomic, environmental, technical, and/or institutional, including ADB's safeguard and other applicable ADB policies. If other outputs are "owned" by other stakeholders, then identify those as well.

(vii) **Review and refine theory of change.** Revise the ToC based on the confirmed project scope. This may involve removing some results chains and revising others.

  (a) Review the ToC from the bottom up asking: "Is this change or condition sufficient for the next one to happen? If not, what is missing?" Add it. "Is this change or condition necessary for the next one to happen?" If not, remove it.

  (b) Ensure cause-and-effect pathways are supported by evidence, including from the

project's economic, and poverty and social analyses, as appropriate. Flag the pathways where further evidence and information are needed and make plans to collect these during project preparation.

  (c) Review assumptions and risks and reconsider unintended consequences and sustainability factors.

(iv) **Finalize project.** Carry out feasibility studies and any other necessary analysis for project preparation. Based on the findings, decide on the most appropriate strategies and results to be pursued under the proposed project. The collective involvement of the borrower, executing agency, other key stakeholders (as appropriate), and ADB is critical at this stage. The final decision should be based on consensus to ensure ownership of the project and to maximize the probability of achieving the desired results. Other issues to keep in mind when finalizing the project include the following.

  (a) Does it conform to local laws, policies, and procedures?

  (b) Are the requisite expertise and capacity available to carry it out?

  (c) Is it affordable and cost-effective, and is the necessary financing available?

  (d) Is it socially acceptable to the target beneficiaries?

  (e) Is it likely to result in any negative externalities that will require mitigation?

  (f) Is it supported by other investments and projects that are ongoing or planned by the government, ADB, or other organizations?

  (g) What are the major risks and how can they be mitigated? Are critical assumptions expected to hold true?

Once the ToC is mapped, the project team will be well-positioned to formulate a good DMF and prepare a relevant detailed project design. The ToC mapping (diagram and narrative) is a working document that can be updated to reflect learning and changes in context over the course of the project cycle.

E. Formulate the Content of the Design and Monitoring Framework

Once the results analysis is finished, the DMF template can be completed by taking the following steps. (Refer to Section II of these guidelines for detailed guidance on each part of the DMF.)

(i) **Develop outcome statement.** Referring to the characteristics of an outcome defined in Box 2, develop the DMF outcome statement. Only one outcome statement should be developed for each project. Ensure it captures the planned change. If working from a ToC diagram, the outcome statement can be developed by selecting an appropriate results statement from the diagram or combining several outcome-level results statements.

(ii) **Clarify impact statements.** Clarify between one and three impact statements the project will be aligned with. Each statement should ideally be sourced from a government national or sector plan.

(iii) **Decide on output statements.** Decide which outputs are necessary and sufficient to achieve the project outcome. Review the DMF results chain logic. Check that there is a strong cause-and-effect relationship between the outputs and outcome (referring to the ToC diagram if prepared).

(iv) **Include critical assumptions and risks.** Add critical assumptions, including assumptions for partner financing, and risks for the two levels of the results chain (activities to outputs and outputs to outcome). Assumptions and risks fill in the cause-and-effect gaps between results levels. If working from a ToC diagram, simply transfer the critical assumption and risk statements into the risk assessment and risk management plan (RAMP) and DMF following the guidance in Section II.D. In addition, any results statements in the ToC that sit between the selected DMF outcome and outputs statements can be converted into assumptions or risks and transferred into the DMF as appropriate. Review the results chain logic, as completing the risks

and critical assumptions column may lead to changes in the DMF results chain.

(v) **Develop performance indicators and set targets.** Include at least one performance indicator for each outcome and output statement. The ToC diagram is a helpful tool for developing performance indicators. Results statements in the ToC that sit between the selected DMF outcome and output statements can inform performance indicators, especially leading indicators of the DMF outcome. Identify targets for each indicator. Ensure outcome-level targets are consistent with the economic and financial analyses (Box 19) and

---

Box 19: Consistency with Economic and Financial Analyses

The economic and financial viability of the project and the sustainability of its benefits are assessed at the design and preparation stage. The assessment is based on the project structure, usually captured in an early draft of the design and monitoring framework (DMF), which identifies, quantifies, and enables the valuation of sustained benefits throughout the working life of the investment.

The DMF outcome statement and the performance indicators and their target values should be aligned with the economic and financial analyses. The target amounts and dates should match the annual benefit stream used in the economic analysis. For example, in an urban rail project, the economic analysis may in part be based on the average daily number of passengers in each year of operation. The benefit stream will include many years of operation in line with the working life of the urban rail system. The DMF outcome indicator will have a target date of the first full year of operation. The target value of the "average daily number of passengers in the first full year of operation" should be the same in the DMF and the economic analysis. There must be consistency between the DMF and the economic analysis for all output and outcome benefits articulated in results statements, indicators, and targets.

realistically achievable within the first the full year of operation following physical completion, or before financial closure of the project. Review the results chain and ensure that the performance indicators measure all dimensions of the corresponding results statement. The selection of performance indicators may lead to reconsideration of the DMF results chain, particularly the outcome statement.

(vi) **List data sources and reporting mechanisms.** For each performance indicator, list the data collection methods to be used for primary data collection and the data sources and reporting mechanisms for secondary data.

(vii) **Determine activities.** Determine the key activities necessary to produce the outputs. Do this sequentially for each output. Agree on milestones for each activity and include them in brackets after each activity description. It is good practice to list key project management activities at the end of the activities row as well.

(viii) **Review results chain logic.** Consideration of the activities may lead to adjustment of the

outputs. In this case, reexamine the full results chain as it may need final adjustment.

(ix) **List inputs.** List the inputs required to carry out the activities by source (e.g., ADB, government, and beneficiaries).

(x) **Specify alignment with Strategy 2030 priorities.** A project's DMF content determines which Strategy 2030 operational priorities (OPs) it is aligned with. Review the DMF performance indicators and tag them to each OP indicator for which the project is expected to contribute results. Below the DMF, list any other OP indicators for which the project is expected to contribute results but for which there are no corresponding DMF performance indicators. Indicate the number of results the project is expected to achieve for each OP indicator, along with notes on the methodology or data source that will be used to report the number of OP results achieved, in the RRP linked document "Contribution to Strategy 2030 Operational Priorities."

IV. Specific Applications of the Design and Monitoring Framework

The basic principles of the DMF are the same across modalities and products, but their application may differ. This section provides guidance on how to prepare a DMF for modalities other than an investment project.

A. Multitranche Financing Facility

The multitranche financing facility (MFF) is a long-term financing instrument that provides assistance through a series of tranches to support a medium- or long-term client investment plan. The facility is composed of a series of separate financing tranches over a fixed period. DMFs are prepared both for the overall facility and for each tranche.[13]

During implementation, the facility DMF should be updated to reflect any changes required as subsequent tranches are approved.[14] For example, the impact statements for the facility and the first tranche should be the same upon their approval, but when the DMF for a subsequent tranche is prepared, the impact statement(s) can be updated to align with the current valid government strategy or plan.

The main DMF issue to be addressed is the relationship between the results chains in the facility DMF and the tranche DMFs, specifically the link between facility outcome and outputs, and tranche outcome and outputs. The sector road map for the facility will guide the specification of the facility outcome and outputs.

With the facility results chain developed, there are two options for the results link between facility and tranches: (i) same level; i.e., facility output = tranche output, facility outcome = tranche outcome; and (ii) cause and effect; i.e., tranche outcome = facility output.

Each MFF team determines which results link option to use based on the design of the facility and tranches. The MFF modality provides flexibility to arrange tranches using multiple designs. As a general rule, prepare the DMFs so that they include indicators measuring achievement of, or progress toward, the facility outcome as soon as beneficial use of outputs can be measured. That may be in one or more tranche DMFs, or only in the facility DMF. Table 4 summarizes the relationship between facility and tranche DMFs for common MFF designs, and the rest of this section presents a project example to illustrate each design. These common designs can be used to determine the appropriate results link, but they are not an exhaustive list of possible MFF designs. Many MFFs employ a combination of designs to arrange tranches—for example, starting with geographic as the first order, followed by component or phase.[15]

Example design 1: Geographic. The facility output amount is typically determined by adding up tranche outputs delivered across different geographic locations in a bottom–up process. This approach is typically used in the urban development, water supply and sanitation, and transport sectors.

---

[13] ADB. 2018. Multitranche Financing Facility. *Operations Manual.* OM D14/BP. Manila. https://www.adb.org/documents/operations-manual.

[14] Change in scope processes for the MFF and individual tranches, including approval authority and reporting, are detailed in Project Administration Instruction 5.02 (ADB. 2018. Change in Loan Projects. *Project Administration Instructions.* PAI 5.02. Manila. https://www.adb.org/documents/project-administration-instructions).

[15] Contracts may be sliced in various ways across the facility period, including by contractual milestones, performance payments, and other measures of contract progress, or on the basis of expected disbursement over a given time period (called "time slices"). The DMF structure is primarily based on when outputs and outcomes will be achieved, not the contract slicing approach used.

Table 4: Common Multitranche Financing Facility Designs—Relationship between Facility and Tranche Design and Monitoring Frameworks

Common MFF Designs	Summary of Relationship between Facility and Tranche DMFs
Tranche outputs are used and benefited from before the final tranche ends | Facility output = tranche output	
1. Geographic	Similar packages of outputs are delivered in different quantities in different locations. Users receive benefits as outputs in a specific geographic location are completed. There is no synergy or interaction between the various locations. The facility output amount is typically determined by adding up tranche outputs delivered across the different geographic locations. The outputs and outcome of the tranches are subsets of the facility outputs and outcome.
2. Phased	A mostly contiguous piece of infrastructure or a large investment program is delivered over time and provides benefits to users before facility completion. The facility DMF output encapsulates the entire infrastructure or program output, while the tranche outputs cover a piece or phase of the overall facility output. Outputs from the first tranches are usable to some extent while the subsequent tranches are still ongoing. The amount of each tranche output is specified from the overall facility output in a top–down process.
3. Financial intermediation	An MFF may include the use of financial intermediary lending as the sole focus of the facility, tranche(s) or as a tranche component, to support sub-loans to eligible sub-borrowers (e.g., homeowners, farmers, business owners). The outputs of a tranche (financing received by beneficiaries) are usable while the subsequent tranches are still planned or ongoing. The tranche outputs are subsets of the facility outputs.
None of the tranche outputs is usable until all tranches have been completed | Facility output = tranche outcome	
4. Component or project	This design is commonly used when the facility output is a large-scale piece of infrastructure or a system. Facility outputs are divided across all tranches, either as separate components or as a series of projects in a sector or in various sectors, and do not deliver benefits to users until all tranches are completed. This design has a cause-and-effect results relationship where all tranche outputs are causally related to facility outputs.

DMF = design and monitoring framework, MFF = multitranche financing facility.

The example in Figure 16 shows the output quantities for water supply and treatment divided over three locations.[16] It shows the same type of output being delivered in different locations, but outputs may vary by location; for example, a water treatment plant in location A, and a network of water distribution lines in location B that are not connected to the treatment plant in location A. There is no synergy or interaction between the various locations. The outputs and outcome of the tranches are subsets of the facility outputs and outcome. The indicators are at the same level between facility and tranche (and are additive).

Table 5 shows the relationship. The results link, shown in blue, is output to output, outcome to outcome.

Example design 2: Phased. A facility with a phased design typically funds a single, large, mostly contiguous piece of infrastructure or a large investment program. The facility DMF output encapsulates the entire infrastructure or program output, while each of the tranche outputs covers a piece or phase of the overall facility output. In the examples of an MFF in the education sector (Figure 17) and road sector (Figure 18), outputs from the first tranche are usable to some

---

[16] The examples of MFF designs in this section are intended to provide illustrative examples for the sole purpose of providing guidance on suitable DMF approaches. They are not intended as guidance for how an MFF should be designed, and they do not represent all possible designs.

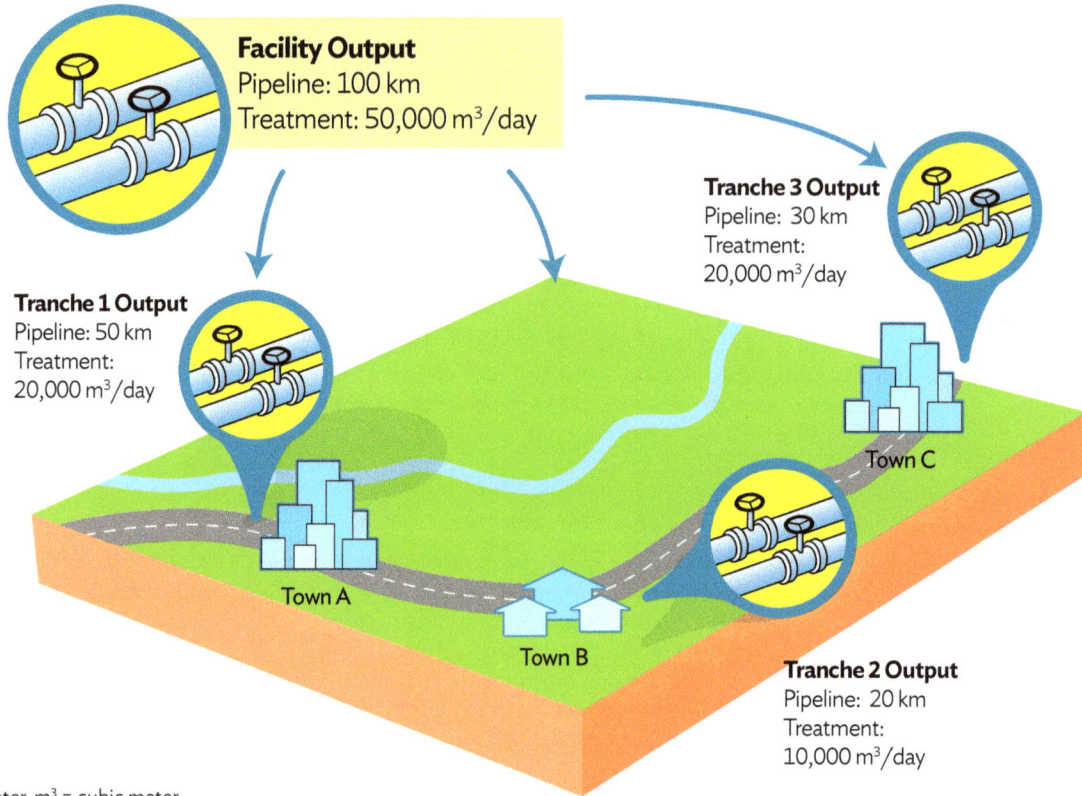

Figure 16: Geographic Design Example—Water Sector

Facility Output
Pipeline: 100 km
Treatment: 50,000 m³/day

Tranche 3 Output
Pipeline: 30 km
Treatment:
20,000 m³/day

Tranche 1 Output
Pipeline: 50 km
Treatment:
20,000 m³/day

Town C

Town A

Town B

Tranche 2 Output
Pipeline: 20 km
Treatment:
10,000 m³/day

km = kilometer, m³ = cubic meter.

Table 5: Geographic Design—Facility and Tranche Relationship for Water Sector

Item	Impacts	Outcome	Outcome Indicator	Outputs	Output Indicators
Facility	Health of residents in two provinces improved (Health Sector Plan, 2014–2020)	Consumption of clean water in towns A, B, and C increased	Targets for combined achievements of all tranches	Water and sanitation infrastructure in towns A, B, and C constructed	100 km of water pipeline laid 50,000 m³/day of water treatment capacity operational
Tranche		Consumption of clean water in town A increased	Subset of facility outcome targets	Water and sanitation infrastructure in town A constructed	50 km of water pipeline laid 20,000 m³/day of water treatment capacity operational

km = kilometer, m³ = cubic meter.

Figure 17: Phased Design Example—Education Sector

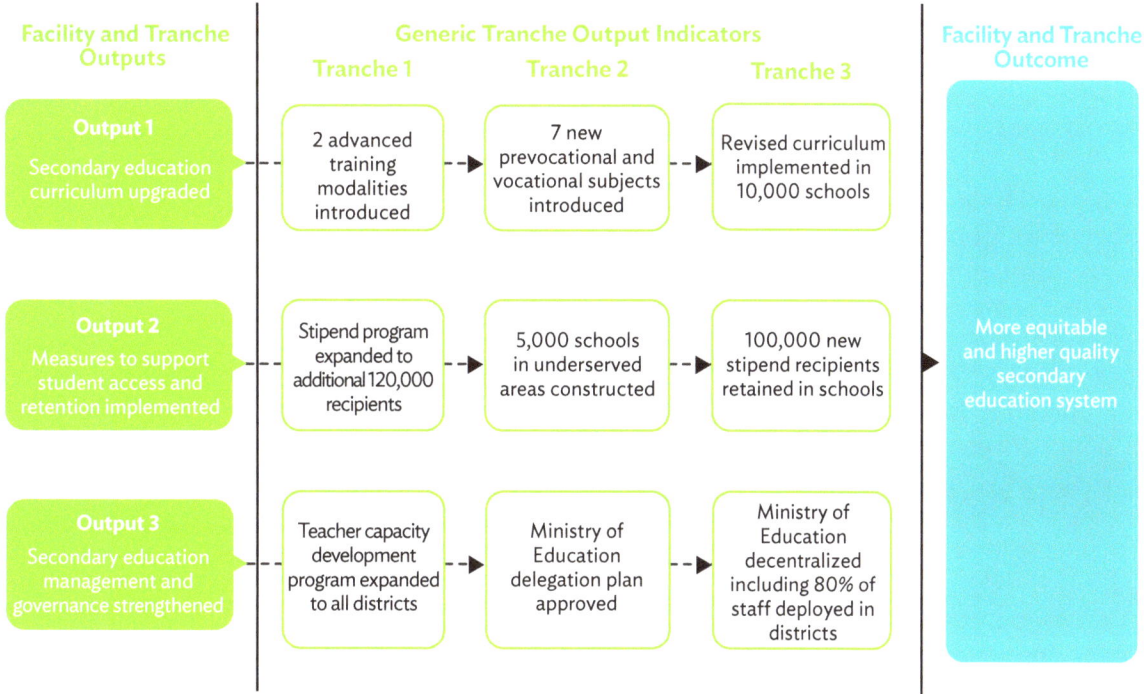

Facility and Tranche Outputs	Generic Tranche Output Indicators			Facility and Tranche Outcome
	Tranche 1	Tranche 2	Tranche 3	
Output 1 Secondary education curriculum upgraded	2 advanced training modalities introduced	7 new prevocational and vocational subjects introduced	Revised curriculum implemented in 10,000 schools	More equitable and higher quality secondary education system
Output 2 Measures to support student access and retention implemented	Stipend program expanded to additional 120,000 recipients	5,000 schools in underserved areas constructed	100,000 new stipend recipients retained in schools	
Output 3 Secondary education management and governance strengthened	Teacher capacity development program expanded to all districts	Ministry of Education delegation plan approved	Ministry of Education decentralized including 80% of staff deployed in districts	

Figure 18: Phased Design Example—Road Sector

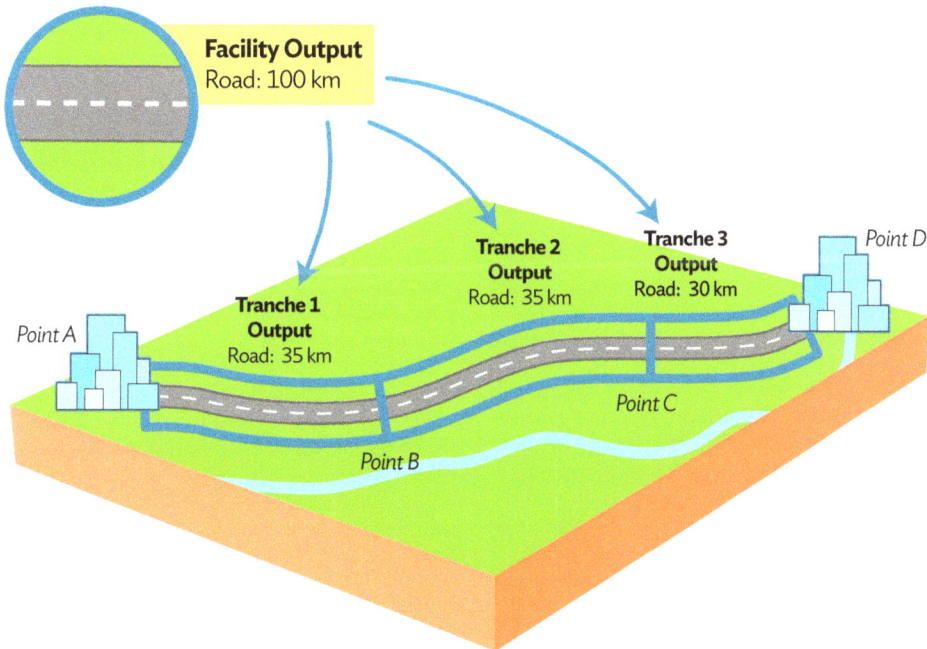

Facility Output
Road: 100 km

Tranche 1 Output
Road: 35 km

Tranche 2 Output
Road: 35 km

Tranche 3 Output
Road: 30 km

Point A

Point B

Point C

Point D

km = kilometer.

extent while the subsequent tranches are still ongoing. The results link between facility and tranche DMFs is output to output—the outputs of the facility and its tranches are at the same results level and the tranche outputs are a subset of the facility outputs. The amount of each tranche output is specified from the overall facility output in a top–down process.

Since the outputs of initial tranches can be used in a beneficial manner (outcome) before all the tranches have been completed, the facility outcome can be at the same level (additive) as the tranche (Figure 18), or the facility outcome may result from synergy among the tranches (Figure 17). In the road sector example (Figure 18) additive facility outcome indicators of (i) travel time between points A and D, (ii) vehicle operating cost along a road from A to D, and (iii) tons per kilometer of freight from A to D may be divided into tranches as follows:

(i)   travel time between points A and B (tranche 1), B and C (tranche 2), and C and D (tranche 3);
(ii)   vehicle operating cost along road from A to B (tranche 1), B to C (tranche 2), and C to D (tranche 3); and
(iii)   tons per km of freight from A to B (tranche 1), B to C (tranche 2), and C to D (tranche 3).

The road sector facility, covering the entire piece of infrastructure, may also have a synergistic outcome that is present only in the final tranche. For example, if there is a manufacturing complex at point A and point D is the border with the neighboring country, then the facility outcome may include manufactured goods crossing the border, which would not be possible until the completion of the third tranche. Table 6 shows the relationship for the road sector example. The results link, shown in blue, is output to output, outcome to outcome. The synergistic outcome is shown in green.

Example design 3: Financial intermediation. An MFF may include the use of financial intermediary lending, as the sole focus of the facility, tranche(s), or as a component of tranche(s), to support sub-loans to eligible sub-borrowers (e.g., homeowners, farmers, and business owners). The tranches can consist of repeated amounts to the same set of financial intermediaries or each tranche can lend to different groups of financial intermediaries and sub-borrowers. The outputs of a tranche are usable while the subsequent tranches are still planned or ongoing. The results link between facility and tranche DMFs is output to output; the outputs of the facility and its tranches are at the same results level and the tranche outputs are a subset of the facility outputs. The amount of each tranche output is specified from the overall facility output in a top–down process. There is typically no synergistic outcome. Table 7 shows an example of a financial intermediation MFF. The results link, shown in blue, is output to output, outcome to outcome.

Table 6: Phased Design—Facility and Tranche Relationship for Road Sector Example

Item	Impact	Outcome	Outcome Indicators	Outputs	Output Indicators
Facility	Value of exports and imports increased by 2017 (Transport Sector Master Plan, 2006)	Additive and/or synergistic (whole more than parts)	Travel time A to D Tons of cross–border cargo	Additive, outputs of all tranches amassed together	100 km of road
Tranche		Subset of facility outcome	Travel time A to B	Subset of facility output	35 km of road

km = kilometer.

Table 7: Financial Intermediation Design—Facility and Tranche Relationship for Solar Rooftop Investment Program Example

Item	Impact	Outcome	Outcome Indicators	Outputs	Output Indicators
Facility	Energy security provided to all in a more environmentally sustainable manner (Integrated Energy Policy, 2020)	Use or application of facility output e.g., Solar rooftop power generating capacity in Country A increased	400 MW of national bank funded solar rooftop power generating capacity installed	Aggregate, outputs of all tranches added up	At least 500 solar rooftop subprojects approved for financing
Tranche		Subset of facility outcome	80 MW of national bank funded solar rooftop power generating capacity	Tranche deliverable e.g., debt funding to the solar rooftop sector increased	At least 100 solar rooftop subprojects approved for financing

MW = megawatt.

Figure 19: Component Design Example—Railway

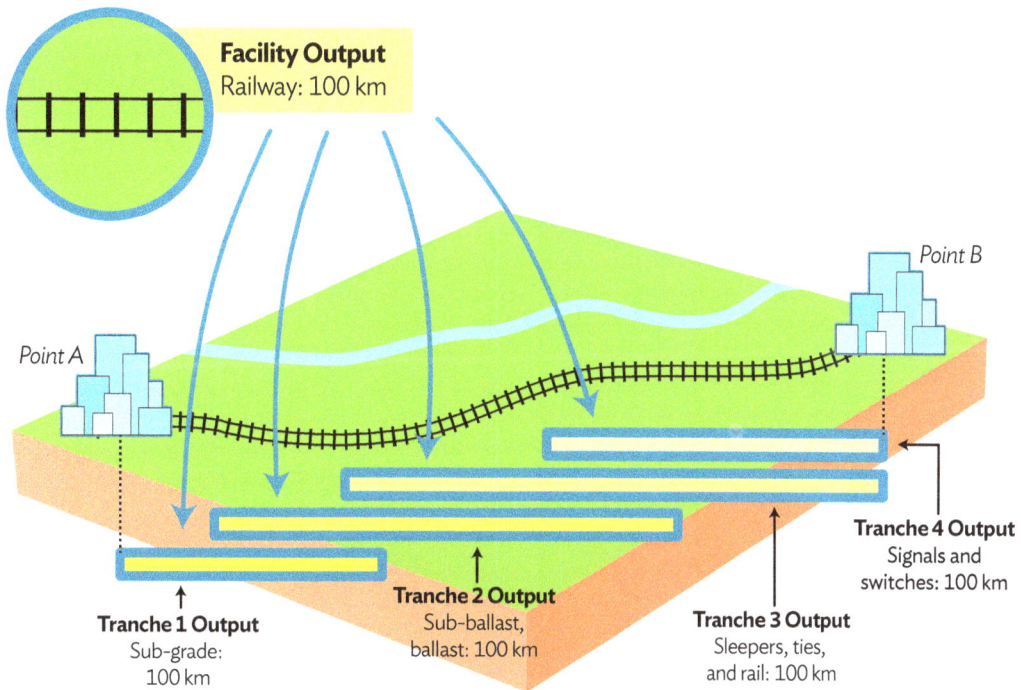

Facility Output
Railway: 100 km

Point B

Point A

Tranche 1 Output
Sub-grade:
100 km

Tranche 2 Output
Sub-ballast,
ballast: 100 km

Tranche 3 Output
Sleepers, ties,
and rail: 100 km

Tranche 4 Output
Signals and
switches: 100 km

km = kilometer.

Example design 4: Component or project. In contrast to the other example designs, none of the tranche outputs is usable until all tranches have been completed. This design is commonly used when the facility output is a large-scale piece of infrastructure or system, and its delivery is divided across all tranches, either as separate components or as one or more projects in a sector or in various sectors. This design uses the cause-and-effect results relationship where all tranche outputs are causally related to facility outputs. In this case, the facility outputs become the outcome for the tranches. In Figure 19, for example, 100 km of railway is divided into components, rather than into contiguous sections. The output of each phase or tranche is 100 km of each constituent part. Only when all the parts are completed can the facility output be achieved (100 km railway from point A to point B operational).

Table 8 shows the relationship. The results link, shown in blue, is facility output to tranche outcome. Each tranche has the same outcome.

B. Results-Based Lending

Under results-based lending (RBL), ADB helps governments design and implement their own programs. ADB links disbursement directly to the achievement of program results. The programs are implemented using the program systems of the developing member country (DMC). RBL operations have a program results framework (PRF) that the government prepares, sometimes with ADB's help. The PRF covers all or part of the overall government-owned sector program and contains a results chain, indicators, and targets. Because the PRF is the government's document, its structure may differ from that of the ADB DMF. A program action plan (PAP) containing selected priority actions is also included in an RBL program. Disbursements are made once the agreed disbursement-linked indicators (DLIs) have been achieved and verified. DLIs are generally a subset of the PRF results indicators.

The RBL PRF and the PAP are parent documents of the RBL DMF. Their relationship is as follows:

(i) All DMF results statements originate from the RBL PRF and the PAP. Ideally, results statements are cited from the PRF, and adjusted, if needed, to align with ADB results chain formulation.
(ii) DMF performance indicators are selected from indicators in the PRF and the PAP. DMF output-level indicators should include DLIs, but they do not all need to be DLIs. It is optional to include DLIs as DMF outcome-level indicators.
(iii) The DMF lists the priority actions from the PAP.

Figure 20 illustrates the process of compiling an RBL DMF.

Table 8: Component Design—Facility and Tranche Relationship for Railway Example

Item	Impact	Outcome	Outcome Indicators	Outputs	Output Indicators
Facility	Value of exports and imports increased by 2024 (Transport Sector Master Plan, 2020)	Use or application of facility output	Ton-km of freight transported	Aggregate, outputs of all tranches combined (top-down)	100 km railway between point A and point B operational
Tranche		Facility output	100 km railway between point A and point B operational	Tranche or contract package deliverable	100 km of subgrade between point A and point B installed

km = kilometer.

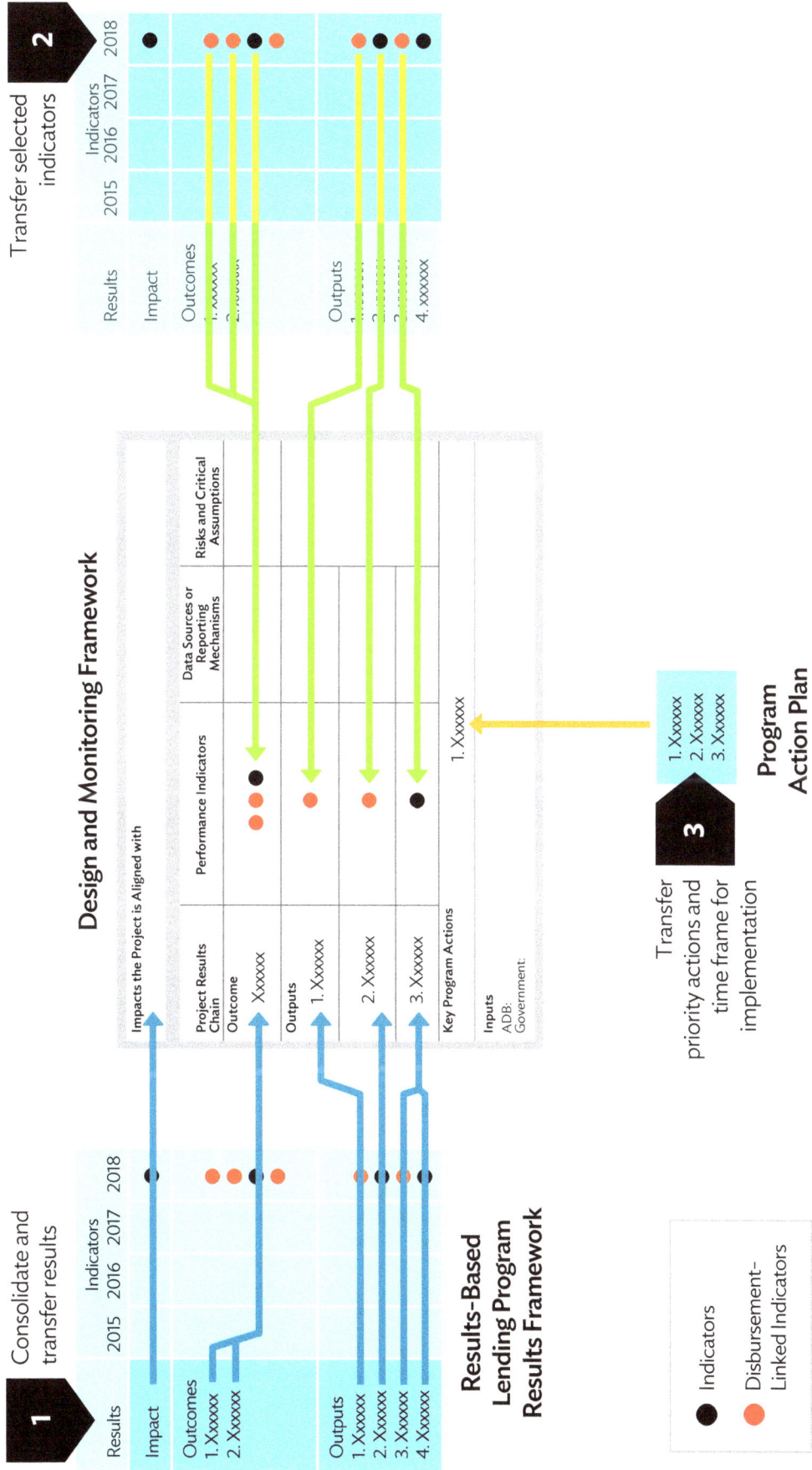

Figure 20: Transferring Results, Indicators, and Key Actions to the Results–Based Lending Design and Monitoring Framework

Figure 21: Policy Design and Monitoring Framework Template

Country's Overarching Development Objective{s}: {Impact Statements(s)}

Outcome: {outcome statement}

Risks and Critical Assumptions: {risks and critical assumptions for achievement of the program outcome}

Prior Actions[a] {subprogram 1 or tranche 1}	**Prior Actions** {subprogram 2 or tranche 2}[b]	**Outcome Indicators**	**Post-Program Partnership Framework**[c]
Reform Area 1: {name of reform area}			
1.1 {description of policy action} 1.2 (etc.)	2.1 {description of policy action} 2.2 (etc.)	a. {performance indicator(s) measuring expected outcome of overall reform program with target and baseline value, and source} b. {performance indicator(s) measuring results most directly attributable to reform area 1, if any}	a.{description of post-program action} b. (etc.)
Reform Area 2: {name of reform area}			
1.3 1.4 (etc.)	2.3 (etc.)	c. {performance indicator(s) measuring results most directly attributable to reform area 2, if any}	c. d. (etc.)
Reform Area 3: {name of reform area}[d]			
1.5 1.6 (etc.)	2.4 (etc.)	c. {performance indicator(s) measuring results most directly attributable to reform area 3, if any}	e. (etc.)

Budget Support
ADB: {amount per subprogam or tranche}
{Name of cofinancier}: {amount per subprogram or tranche}

ADB = Asian Development Bank.

[a] The column heading "prior actions" is used for completed subprograms or tranches, while the heading "policy action" is used for forthcoming subprogram or tranches. Prior actions should be written in past tense while policy actions should be written in future tense.

[b] Columns added or deleted based on number of subprograms or tranches.

[c] Optional column.

[d] Rows added or deleted based on number of reform areas.

C.   Policy-Based Lending

Policy-based lending (PBL) facilitates the implementation of sector and intersectoral policy reforms in a DMC. All types of conventional PBL include a policy design and monitoring framework (PDMF),[17] which has a unique design suited to the PBL modality (Figure 21).

The PDMF sets out the overall objectives of the program, the reforms already completed under the program ("prior actions"), the planned reforms ("policy actions") and their timing, the risks and critical assumptions, and the expected outcome of the reform program. Outcome indicators are presented in SMART format aligned with the most relevant program reform area. A post-program partnership framework may also be included to further strengthen the sustainability of the reforms initiated (footnote 17).

The results chain for PBL should be based on the actions to be undertaken by the government as part of the reforms, as follows:

(i)   The country's overarching development objective is the end benefit of the reform that the PBL is aligned with.

(ii)   The outcome describes the expected benefits from the completion of the policy actions undertaken under the reform program. A good outcome statement captures the breadth of the reforms and is a direct result of the completed policy actions.

(iii)   Reform areas are a summary description of the areas (e.g., substantive legal, institutional, or

Table 9: Examples of Policy-Based Lending Results Chains

Item	Results Chain	
	Reform Area	Outcome
Generic examples	Means to reduce constraints established or implemented	Constraints reduced
	Policy conditions established or implemented	Effects of policy conditions
	Barriers removed	Effects of barrier removal
	Measures to mitigate negative effects of reforms on population groups approved or undertaken	Negative effects on population groups mitigated
	Systems to implement reforms strengthened	Effects of reforms
	Decisions, procedures, decrees, regulations, legislation, processes, plans, laws, policies, or amendments thereof, established, approved, and/or issued	Effects of these measures being undertaken—medium-term reform results
Specific examples	Government legislation addressing nonperforming loans of banks approved	Nonperforming loans reduced
	Cost recovery increased, subsidies reduced, interest rates rationalized	Competition and private sector involvement increased
	Enabling institutional and policy environment for financial inclusion strengthened	Financial inclusion increased

---

[17]   ADB. 2020. Policy-Based Lending. *Operations Manual*. OM D4/BP. Manila. https://www.adb.org/documents/operations-manual.

regulatory reforms) that the policy actions taken under the program are designed to improve.

Table 9 shows generic and specific examples of common PBL results chains.

Completed policy actions, referred to as "prior actions," are stated in the PDMF grouped by reform area, and the expected outcome of the reform program is measured using SMART indicators. The indicators are ideally direct measures of the outcome, but suitable leading and proxy indicators may also be used. In addition to indicators that measure the overall program outcome, indicators that measure immediate and direct results of a specific series of policy actions within a reform area should also be included, as relevant. Their inclusion can help measure and demonstrate the criticality of a specific reform area and series of policy actions.

Risks and critical assumptions that would affect achievement of the program outcome, even if all policy actions are successfully completed, are recorded in the PDMF. "Lack of government commitment" is not a suitable risk for PBL because government commitment to the reform program is a prerequisite for selecting the modality.

There are two general categories of PBL: conventional and crisis response. A PDMF is required for all conventional PBL. PDMF development and the results chain will differ slightly depending on the PBL type.

Conventional policy-based lending. Conventional PBL includes the following subtypes:

- **Stand-alone.** This type of PBL may have a single tranche or multiple tranches, but only one PDMF is prepared. The results chain for stand-alone, single-tranche PBL follows the examples in Table 9. For stand-alone PBL with multiple tranches, the outcome indicators and policy actions under each reform area are expected to be achieved and measurable within 12 months after the program implementation period has been completed.
- **Programmatic approach.** This type of PBL can have two or more subprograms, but only one PDMF is prepared for the full program and this is updated

as each subprogram is approved. The results chain follows the examples in Table 9. Outcome indicators are for the entire program and should be achieved and measurable within 12 months after implementation of the final subprogram has been completed. The following steps describe the PDMF content at each approval stage.

(i) The concept paper includes a preliminary PDMF that identifies at least the tentative outcome for the overall program and indicative policy actions for subprogram 1. Tentative policy actions for subsequent subprograms are included if known.

(ii) The RRP for subprogram 1 presents the overall PBL program and subprogram 1 for approval. At this stage, the PDMF presents the program results chain, outcome indicators, risks and critical assumptions, final policy actions for subprogram 1, and tentative policy actions for all subsequent subprograms. Tentative policy actions for subsequent subprograms are included if known.

(iii) From subprogram 2 onward, the RRP includes an updated PDMF for the program that (i) confirms the prior actions for the proposed subprogram; (ii) documents achievement to date against outcome indicators for which data are available; and (iii) identifies any updates to the PDMF, such as new indicators added to more fully measure the outcome of the final reform program, or existing outcome indicators revised to reflect the current program context (e.g., setting a higher target if the original outcome has already been met mid-program). Any adjustments to the PDMF from subprogram 2 onward, excluding updates to policy actions, should be flagged and explained in a footnote below the PDMF.

- **Contingent disaster financing.** Contingent disaster financing is a mechanism designed to provide budgetary support for DMCs in the event of a disaster triggered by a natural hazard. The PDMF is prepared based on the guidance for stand-alone PBL and must also include a post-programmatic partnership framework. The content of the PDMF should reflect this type of financing's focus on strengthening the legal, institutional, and policy frameworks to enhance preparedness for and response to such disasters. Outcome indicators measure improved disaster preparedness and response.

- **Policy-based guarantee.** Policy-based guarantees are guarantees that support commercial lenders' financing to the government. The PDMF is developed according to whether it is designed as a stand-alone or programmatic approach. The expected outcome indicators for a policy-based guarantee measure the benefit from the legal, institutional, and regulatory reforms undertaken as part of the program; and, if relevant, the benefits derived from use of the ADB partial credit guarantee instrument, such as the reduction in government borrowing costs from commercial markets.

Crisis-response policy-based lending. This includes special PBL and the countercyclical support facility. Given its crisis-response nature, a stand-alone DMF may be prepared in lieu of a PDMF. Typically, the PDMF or DMF will not link to sector results because these types of support are usually neither predicted nor planned (footnote 17).

When transaction TA is provided to support the achievement of PBL results, the transaction TA outputs are usually already reflected in the key policy actions identified in the PDMF. However, in exceptional cases where the transaction TA will deliver key outputs or outcomes that are not already captured in the PDMF of the associated PBL, these are measured by adding indicators to the PDMF.

D. Technical Assistance

There are two types of TA: knowledge and support TA and transaction TA.

Knowledge and support technical assistance. Knowledge and support TA is stand-alone TA that is not directly linked to other ADB-financed projects. It can be used for purposes such as developing capacity; providing policy and technical advice; and generating, disseminating, and using knowledge. Knowledge and support TA requires its own DMF.

The knowledge and support TA completion report is circulated within 6 months of the TA financial closing date. Therefore, the outcome indicators should measure short-term outcomes or use leading indicators, which measure preliminary indications of the outcome.

Depending on the design of the knowledge and support TA, the impact statement(s) may not reach as high as sector results and may therefore be defined by the project or sourced from an institutional strategy instead of from a national development or sector strategy. The same applies for regional knowledge and support TA impact statement(s), which may link to the regional or subregional strategy, plan, or framework of a regional organization (including ADB); or, possibly, to another type of higher-level strategy, such as a United Nations agreement.

Transaction technical assistance. Transaction TA either (i) directly benefits a project that is, or will be, financed by ADB, for example by providing project preparation and/or project implementation capacity support, or policy advice in preparation for PBL; or (ii) helps develop a public–private partnership (PPP) as part of transaction advisory services. Transaction TA, including transaction TA cluster and facility, does not have its own DMF. Rather, any significant final results delivered by the transaction TA are integrated into the DMF(s) of the related sovereign operation(s). The significance of the results of the transaction TA for the operation(s) it relates to determines which of the following options is used for integrating transaction TA results into the associated operation's DMF.

(i) **No incorporation required.** If the transaction TA is not expected to deliver any results that are considered significant final results in the context of the DMF results chain of the associated operation, then no results statements or indicators specific to the transaction TA are integrated into the DMF of the associated operation. This is the case, for example, where the transaction TA's outputs are focused on project preparation or will help deliver the associated project's outputs but are not major final outputs in the context of the associated operation.

(ii) **Output-level integration.** If the transaction TA's outputs constitute a significant and

unique output in the context of the associated operation, then an output statement specific to the transaction TA and one or more performance indicators are added to the DMF of the associated operation (Figure 22). The output statement is a summary statement that encapsulates the transaction TA outputs consistent with the TA report. This level of integration is relevant, for example, if the

---

Figure 22: Options for Output-Level Integration of Transaction Technical Assistance into Design and Monitoring Framework of Associated Operation

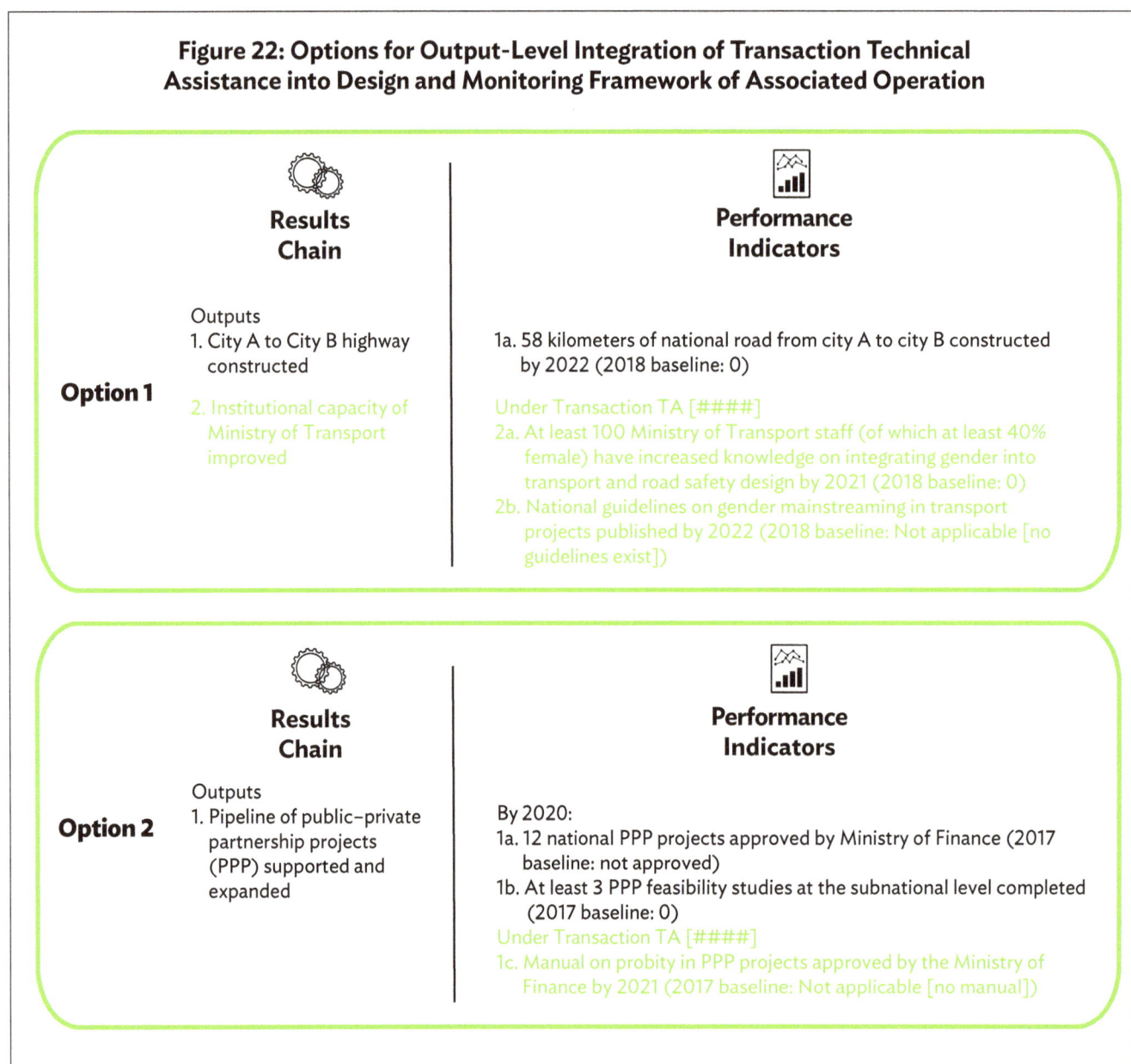

Option 1

Results Chain

Outputs
1. City A to City B highway constructed

2. Institutional capacity of Ministry of Transport improved

Performance Indicators

1a. 58 kilometers of national road from city A to city B constructed by 2022 (2018 baseline: 0)

Under Transaction TA [####]
2a. At least 100 Ministry of Transport staff (of which at least 40% female) have increased knowledge on integrating gender into transport and road safety design by 2021 (2018 baseline: 0)
2b. National guidelines on gender mainstreaming in transport projects published by 2022 (2018 baseline: Not applicable [no guidelines exist])

Option 2

Results Chain

Outputs
1. Pipeline of public–private partnership projects (PPP) supported and expanded

Performance Indicators

By 2020:
1a. 12 national PPP projects approved by Ministry of Finance (2017 baseline: not approved)
1b. At least 3 PPP feasibility studies at the subnational level completed (2017 baseline: 0)
Under Transaction TA [####]
1c. Manual on probity in PPP projects approved by the Ministry of Finance by 2021 (2017 baseline: Not applicable [no manual])

transaction TA will deliver institutional capacity building outputs that are considered significant final outputs in the context of the associated operation (Figure 22, Option 1). If the associated operation's DMF already contains an output statement that captures the transaction TA output, one or more performance indicators specific to the transaction TA are inserted under the relevant output statement(s) in the main operation's DMF (Figure 22, Option 2). The output and/or indicator(s) should be preceded by a heading such as "Under Transaction TA [####]," to distinguish the transaction TA's output and/or indicator(s) from those of the associated operation.

(iii) **Outcome-level integration.** If the transaction TA is expected to achieve a unique and significant outcome-level result that aligns with the outcome of the associated operation, an outcome indicator specific to the transaction TA can be included in the associated operation's DMF. For example, replication or scale-up of a technology or approach piloted by the TA.

(iv) **Activities and inputs integration.** The transaction TA's budget, financier, and source of funds is added to the DMF of the associated operation. As relevant, the transaction TA's activities, or a summary of these, can be added as well.

For transaction TA approved before or alongside its associated operation(s), transaction TA results can be incorporated into the associated operation's DMF as it is developed. For transaction TA associated with an operation already under implementation, transaction TA results are added to the associated operation's DMF through a change-in-scope process. This can be done either at midterm review or during any review period before project closing.

Common technical assistance results chains. The TA projects that ADB typically finances can be grouped into three general focuses: providing policy and technical advice; supporting capacity development; and promoting knowledge generation, dissemination, and use. A single TA project design may include one or more of these general focuses.

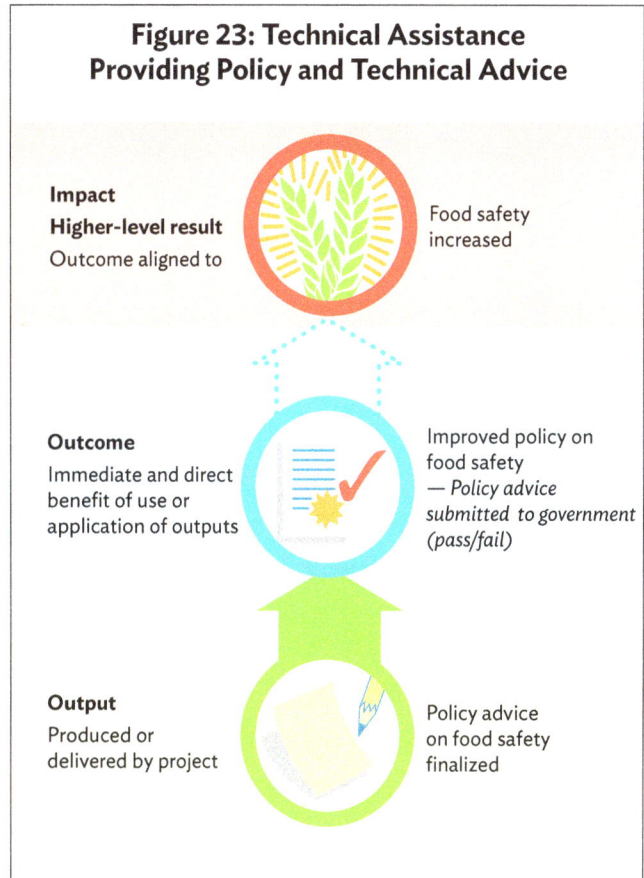

Figure 23: Technical Assistance Providing Policy and Technical Advice

Impact
Higher-level result
Outcome aligned to — Food safety increased

Outcome
Immediate and direct benefit of use or application of outputs — Improved policy on food safety — *Policy advice submitted to government (pass/fail)*

Output
Produced or delivered by project — Policy advice on food safety finalized

For TA focusing on providing policy and technical advice, recipient governments consider the advice for adoption and implementation. Figure 23 shows a typical results chain for TA providing policy and technical advice, with a leading outcome indicator measuring preliminary indications of use.

For TA providing capacity development, the results chain is significantly different depending on whether the recipient of capacity development is an organization or individuals (who may be from multiple organizations). The results chain will also differ depending on whether the capacity development involves assistance in implementation. This can be thought of as the difference between "hand over," with no assistance for implementation; and "hand-holding," where implementation is assisted on an ongoing basis. Training is usually "hand over," while implementation assistance is usually "hand-holding." Table 10 captures these differences.

Specific Applications of the DMF

Table 10: Capacity Development Recipients and Implementation Support

Item	No Implementation Support (Hand Over)		With Implementation Support (Hand-Holding)	
	Outputs	Outcome	Outputs	Outcome
Organization recipient	Models, manuals, guidelines, regulations, processes, systems, plans, policies, etc. produced. Knowledge and skills enhanced	Models, manuals, etc., applied, implemented, undertaken, enacted, enforced, etc. Knowledge and skills applied	Models, manuals, etc., produced and implemented Knowledge and skills enhanced and applied	Overall performance of organization enhanced
Individual recipients	Knowledge and skills enhanced	Knowledge and skills applied	Knowledge and skills enhanced and applied	Overall performance of individuals enhanced

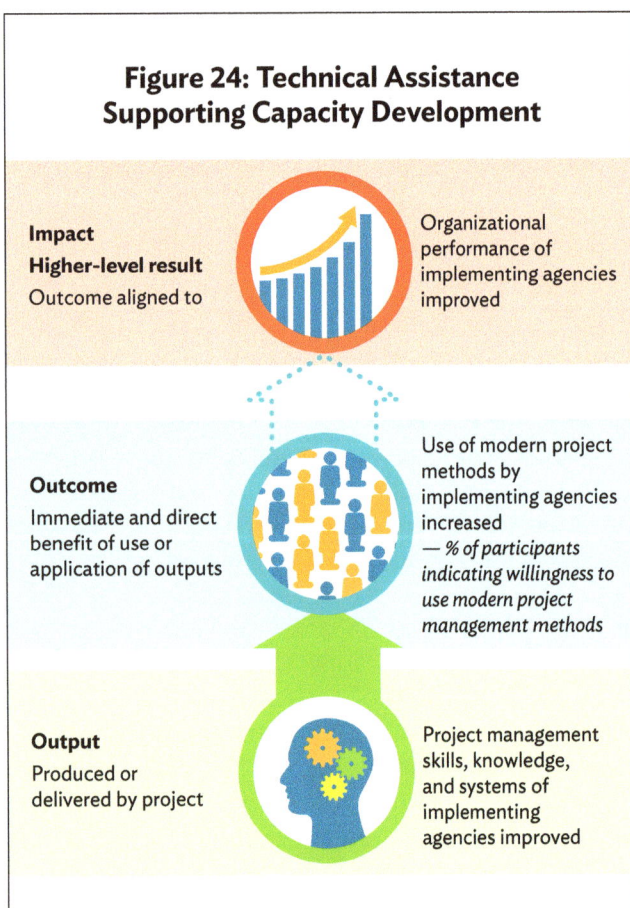

Figure 24: Technical Assistance Supporting Capacity Development

Impact
Higher-level result
Outcome aligned to

Organizational performance of implementing agencies improved

Outcome
Immediate and direct benefit of use or application of outputs

Use of modern project methods by implementing agencies increased
— % of participants indicating willingness to use modern project management methods

Output
Produced or delivered by project

Project management skills, knowledge, and systems of implementing agencies improved

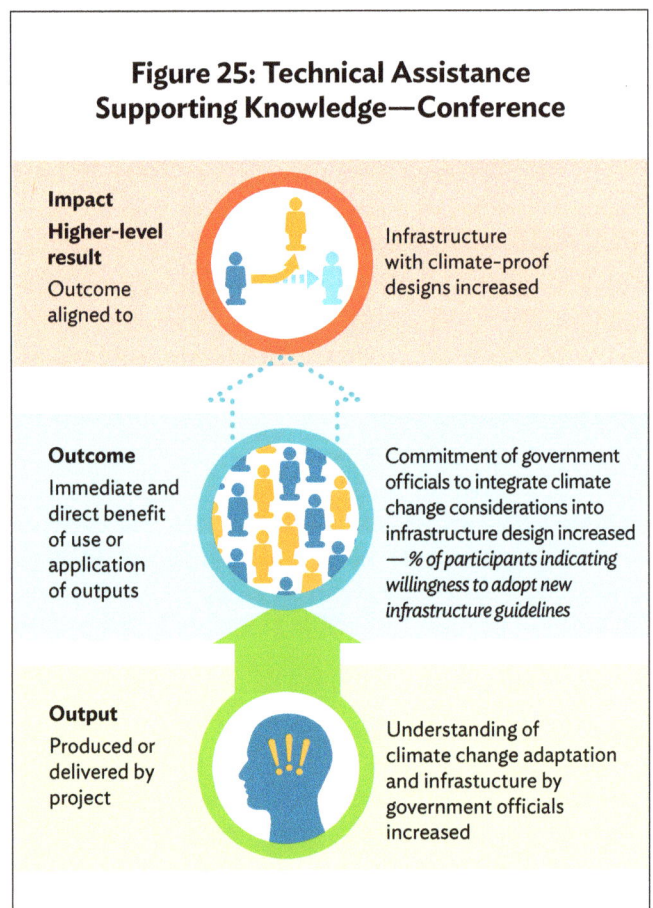

Figure 25: Technical Assistance Supporting Knowledge—Conference

Impact
Higher-level result
Outcome aligned to

Infrastructure with climate-proof designs increased

Outcome
Immediate and direct benefit of use or application of outputs

Commitment of government officials to integrate climate change considerations into infrastructure design increased
— % of participants indicating willingness to adopt new infrastructure guidelines

Output
Produced or delivered by project

Understanding of climate change adaptation and infrastructure by government officials increased

Figure 24 shows a typical results chain for a TA providing capacity development, with a leading outcome indicator measuring likelihood of knowledge and skills application.

Some TA projects are concerned with knowledge generation, and its dissemination to and use by a variety of audiences. Figure 25 shows a typical results chain for knowledge dissemination through a conference,

Table 11: Suggested Generic Indicators for Knowledge and Skills Enhancement

✘ Do not use by itself—Only measures activity and not a meaningful result	✔ Use—Measures learning
Number of training events or conferences held	Number or percentage of participants passing test
Number of people that attended a conference or workshop	Number or percentage of participants reporting improved awareness, knowledge, or skills in subject area(s) (ideally via a survey)
Number of person-days of training delivered	Number or percentage of participants demonstrating improved awareness, knowledge, or skills in subject area(s) (typically as assessed by the trainer or a subject-matter expert)

with a leading outcome indicator measuring likelihood of application of knowledge. Indicators for TA that supports research and development can be drawn from the ADB guidelines, *Crafting a Knowledge Management Results Framework*.[18]

Indicators for capacity development and knowledge-focused TA projects should measure knowledge and skills enhanced at the output level. Table 11 contains generic indicators of knowledge and skills enhancement.

Technical assistance cluster. A TA cluster embodies the same types of results chain as its component TA projects, so it is not considered a distinct type of TA for DMF purposes. However, since a cluster is composed of subprojects, each subproject of a knowledge and support TA cluster has a separate DMF. The relationships between the overall cluster results and those of each subproject follow the same link as MFFs and are either cluster output to subproject output (Figures 26 and 27) or cluster output to subproject outcome (Figure 28). Impacts are the same for the cluster and all subprojects. In Figure 26, a single cluster output is divided across three subprojects. In Figure 27, each cluster output is assigned to a separate subproject.

E. Other Modalities and Products

Sector loans. Sector loans are used to finance many subprojects in the sector or subsector in support of

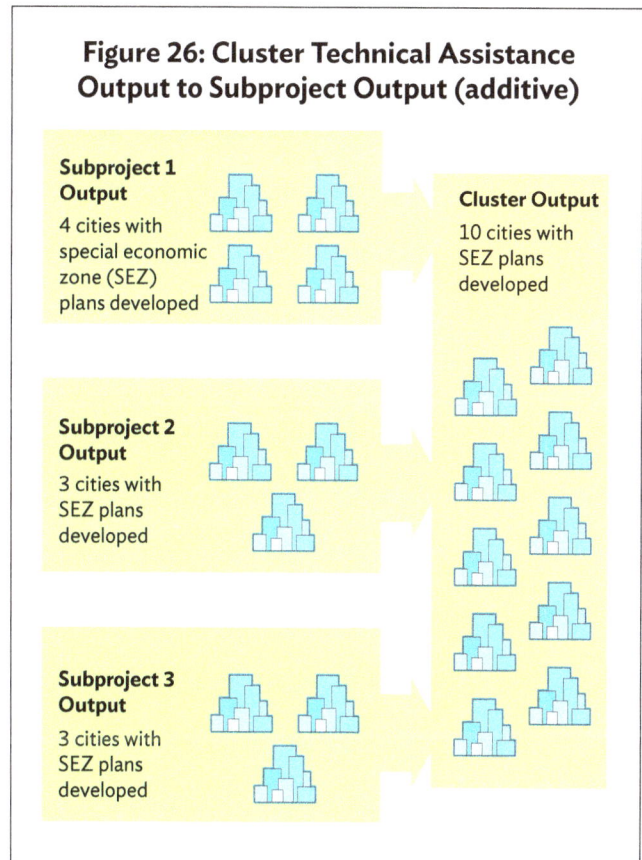

Figure 26: Cluster Technical Assistance Output to Subproject Output (additive)

Subproject 1 Output
4 cities with special economic zone (SEZ) plans developed

Subproject 2 Output
3 cities with SEZ plans developed

Subproject 3 Output
3 cities with SEZ plans developed

Cluster Output
10 cities with SEZ plans developed

the sector development plan. The sector or subsector development plan informs the DMF outcome and indicators. Each subproject deliverable or cluster of subproject deliverables represents an output in the sector loan's DMF.

18 ADB. 2010. *Crafting a Knowledge Management Results Framework*. Manila. https://www.adb.org/sites/default/files/publication/27576/crafting-knowledge-management-results-framework.pdf.

Figure 27: Cluster Outputs Assigned to Subprojects (additive)

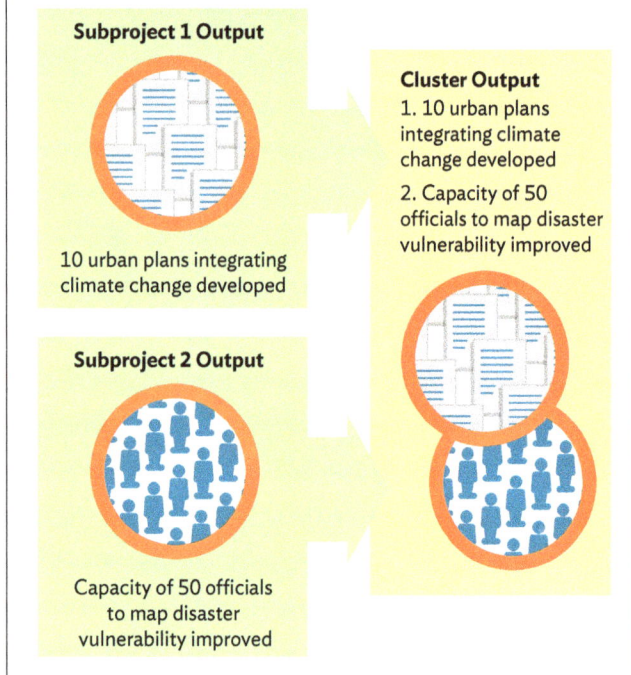

Subproject 1 Output

10 urban plans integrating climate change developed

Subproject 2 Output

Capacity of 50 officials to map disaster vulnerability improved

Cluster Output

1. 10 urban plans integrating climate change developed

2. Capacity of 50 officials to map disaster vulnerability improved

Sector development program. A single DMF is approved for both the PBL and investment loans. It is a hybrid of an investment operation DMF and a PDMF. The outcome level includes performance indicators for the completed sector development program. The reform areas and output level of the DMF includes key policy actions of the PBL program (as per guidance in Section IV.C) and output indicators for the investment loan. Key activities of the investment loan are listed with milestones.

Emergency assistance loans. Emergency assistance loans are generally treated like project loans and therefore require a DMF. Their outputs generally include mitigation of immediate losses to high-priority assets, capacity, or productivity; and may involve rebuilding high-priority physical assets; restoring economic, social, and governance activities after emergencies; and/or increasing the capacity and resilience of infrastructure and systems during a longer-term emergency such as a pandemic.

Figure 28: Subproject Output to Cluster Output (causal)

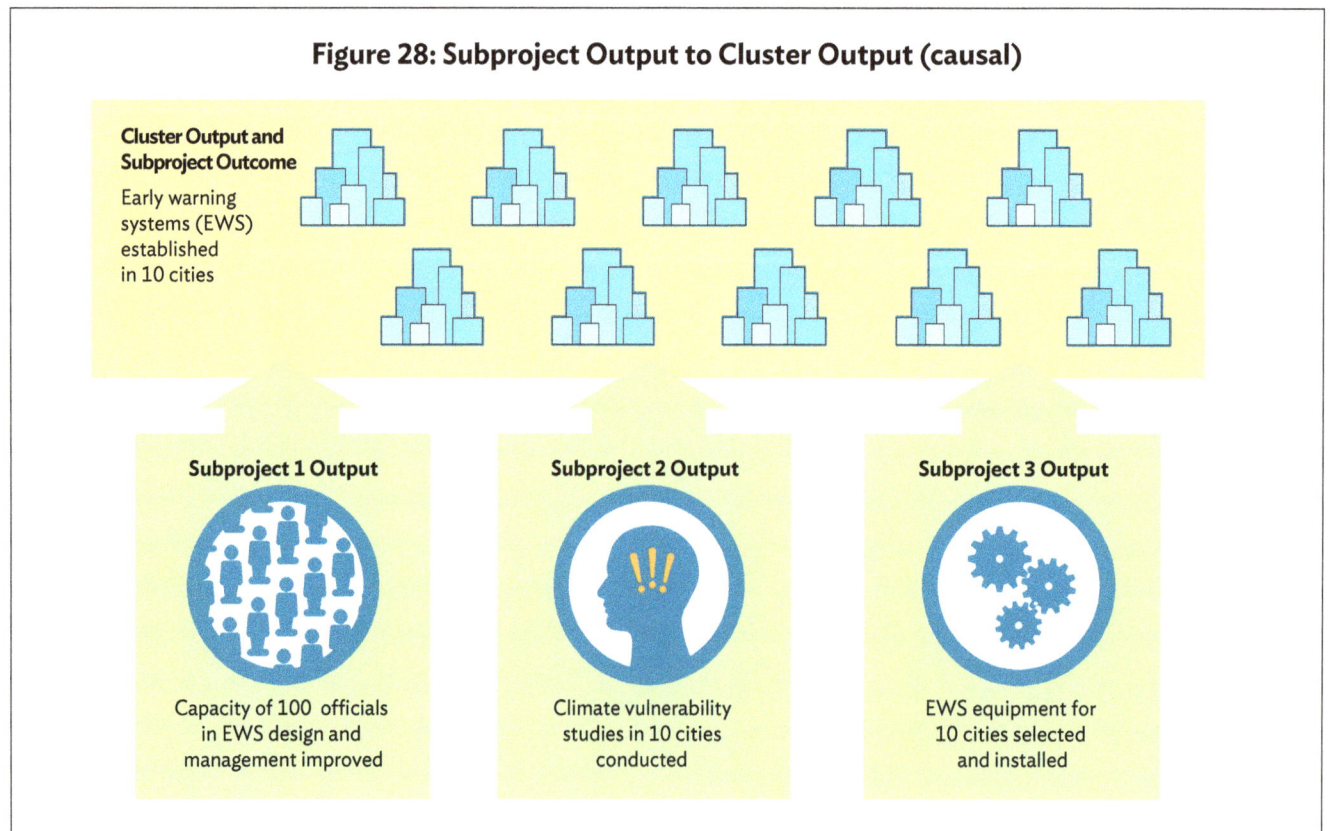

Cluster Output and Subproject Outcome

Early warning systems (EWS) established in 10 cities

Subproject 1 Output

Capacity of 100 officials in EWS design and management improved

Subproject 2 Output

Climate vulnerability studies in 10 cities conducted

Subproject 3 Output

EWS equipment for 10 cities selected and installed

Small expenditure financing facility. The small expenditure financing facility finances multiple small activities to prepare or support ADB-financed projects. There is no facility DMF, rather each activity report contains a DMF that includes only activities and outputs with associated performance indicators which should align with the outcome and/or output(s) of the linked ADB-financed project(s).

Project readiness financing facility. The project readiness financing facility is used to develop projects and make them ready for implementation by the time they are approved. The facility's outputs and activities are specified in the facility approval documents but the facility does not have its own DMF because its activities and outputs lead to the development of operations with their own DMF.

Public–private partnership standby financing facility. The PPP standby financing facility is a pilot modality introduced in 2018 that supports PPP projects from sovereign operations for which the government owes a financial obligation over a long concession period. The business processes for this modality are under development and it remains to be determined whether a DMF will be required.

V. Using the Design and Monitoring Framework during Implementation and at Completion

A. Results Monitoring and Evaluation Arrangements

Results monitoring and evaluation (M&E) are integral to managing for development results and good project management generally. Information produced through these processes is essential to those managing and overseeing project implementation. It is also used to meet reporting accountabilities to a variety of stakeholders (including ADB, DMCs, investors, development partners, and civil society) about progress and performance, and is a means to support organizational learning and continuous improvement.

M&E are two complementary but distinct processes (Table 12).

In addition to a good DMF, a strong M&E plan consists of four key elements: clear activity planning, precise designation of roles, quality assurance plans, and budget allocations (Box 20). The M&E plan for sovereign operations is outlined in the project administration manual (PAM).

Results monitoring responsibilities. The borrower, typically via its implementing agency, is responsible for collecting results data, and reporting and using

Table 12: Project Results Monitoring and Evaluation at ADB: What, Why, When, and by Whom?

Item	Project Results Monitoring	Project Evaluation	
What?	Tracking inputs, activities, outputs, outcomes, and other aspects of the project	Assessment of the extent of results achievement and implementation performance along some key dimensions	
	Focuses mainly on delivery of activities and outputs; monitoring risks, assumptions, and for unintended effects; and, most importantly, tracking progress toward the intended outcome	Focuses on both expected and achieved outcome, examining results chains, implementation processes, contextual factors, and causality	
Why?	To ensure successful project implementation	To understand the range of factors that contribute to or constrain the achievement of results, to learn, and for accountability	
When?	Continuously throughout project implementation as an integral part of project management and supervision	At specific points during project implementation (e.g., a midterm evaluation), at completion, and/or post-completion	
By whom?	Implementing and executing agencies in developing member countries, ADB project administration team, and sometimes by an independent monitor (e.g., for results-based lending)	**Self-Evaluation**	**Independent Evaluation**
		A unit or individuals reporting to the management of the funder, partner, or implementing organization; e.g., implementing and executing agencies in developing member countries, ADB project administration team, or consultants hired by these	Entities and individuals free from the control of those responsible for the design and implementation of the project, such as ADB's Independent Evaluation Department

ADB = Asian Development Bank.

Box 20: Key Elements of a Strong Monitoring and Evaluation Plan

(i) **Clear activity planning (including timelines) for data collection, analysis, and reporting.** Information produced is relevant, timely, and responds to the needs of different users (e.g., project management, developing member countries, the Asian Development Bank, and intended project beneficiaries).

(ii) **Clear designation of roles and responsibilities.** Key stakeholders are actively involved in planning, collecting, reviewing, and interpreting performance information to the extent possible. Project monitoring arrangements are integrated into the developing member country's existing management systems. Roles and responsibilities are clearly outlined in the consultants' terms of reference.

(iii) **Quality assurance plans.** Capacity is in place for collecting, analyzing, verifying, and reporting timely and valid performance information.

(iv) **Budget allocations covering anticipated costs.** Requisite monitoring and evaluation costs are budgeted for in the project management and administration budget line and detailed in the project administration manual.

the information for monitoring purposes during implementation.[19] In addition to its own monitoring activities, the ADB project team relies on the borrower's reports to monitor progress and inform management. Therefore, ADB must ensure that adequate results monitoring arrangements are in place. Results monitoring arrangements proposed during project preparation need to reflect the borrower's institutional capacity and address any issues related to staffing, processes, accountabilities and responsibilities, knowledge, skills, equipment, and budget required to carry out this monitoring function. As part of its

design, a project can include an explicit component for improving the borrower's results monitoring capacity, or ADB can support this via a wider institutional capacity development initiative. Production of statistical information is essential, but it is equally important to develop the capacity to use this data in planning and decision-making. Larger projects may need an M&E specialist on the project implementation team.

Planning for self-evaluations. This guidance focuses specifically on self-evaluation (refer to Table 12 for the distinction between self- and independent evaluation). During the project design phase, project teams should prepare for planned and potential self-evaluations by ensuring that they are adequately budgeted for and that the baseline data and any additional information that may be required will be available to evaluators at the appropriate time.

- **When to conduct additional self-evaluations.** In addition to the mandatory self-evaluations (project completion report [PCR] and TA completion report), it may be worthwhile conducting more in-depth self-evaluations to help better understand what is working well for the project, what is not, and why, and gain insights about how to improve current and future projects. This may take the form of a midterm self-evaluation or an impact evaluation study.
  - A **midterm self-evaluation** can help the project team identify and understand issues in design, implementation, and management, and devise appropriate actions to address them. This is a deeper investigation into project performance and questions of interest to project management than that undertaken during a standard ADB midterm review, and can be particularly useful for complex and problem projects.
  - It may be worth investing in an **impact evaluation** study to more rigorously understand what works and how by measuring which changes are attributable to a project, especially for innovative project designs that do not yet have a record of

---

[19] ADB. 2013. Bank Policy on Project Performance Management System. *Operations Manual.* OM Section J1/BP. Manila. https://www.adb.org/documents/operations-manual.

success and for designs being considered for expansion or replication. Impact evaluation methods are often needed to test whether critical assumptions in the project's theory of change held true in practice and identify unintended effects.[20]

- **Budgeting for self-evaluation.** Budgets vary based on the self-evaluation's scale and location, the cost of experts, and the level of complexity of the methodologies and data collection tools required to answer the chosen evaluation questions. These costs will vary based on local capacity and availability of data. An under-resourced self-evaluation risks being a suboptimal investment. ADB has TA funds to resource impact evaluations. Transaction TA funds can be used to fund self-evaluation activities conducted during the project design phase (e.g., evaluation design planning and baseline studies). It is advisable to include the necessary consultants (e.g., PCR consultants and survey specialists) in the project implementation budget. The PAM should detail the budget and other key information about the required self-evaluations and any additional self-evaluations ADB and the DMC agree to conduct, including draft consultant terms of reference.

There are numerous research tools and methods for collecting information to support project monitoring and enrich self-evaluations.[21] Project teams can consult ADB's Economic Research and Regional Cooperation Department for guidance on designing and funding impact evaluations, and the Independent Evaluation Department for general guidance on evaluation designs and methodologies.

B.   Implementation

The DMF is a core element of ADB's project performance management system. Regularly collecting data on the project's performance indicators throughout the implementation period provides managers and stakeholders with up-to-date information on progress toward the desired outcome. This enables managers to identify strengths and problems as they occur so that they can take timely corrective action to best ensure the intended outcome is achieved.

ADB's supervision role involves providing technical guidance and operational supervision to projects under implementation. ADB staff monitor the projects based on their DMFs by reviewing reports, conducting site visits, cross-referencing with other stakeholders, and/or sometimes by hiring external monitors. Candid and timely monitoring of a project's DMF is essential to alert the borrower, cofinanciers, managers, and concerned ADB staff about any issues that may arise during implementation and take any proactive measures needed, such as project restructuring, to enhance the likelihood of the project meeting its objectives.

Incorporating monitoring and evaluation into project launch activities. After project approval and signing of the legal agreements, the ADB project team works with the borrower to ensure that the required M&E systems are in place. During the project inception mission, the ADB project team should meet with executing and implementing agency staff and other key stakeholders to review and discuss the DMF bearing in mind that there are likely to be new staff in the project implementation unit and other new key stakeholders who were not involved in designing the project. It is important to ensure all key stakeholders clearly understand and agree on the project's objectives and how success will be measured. The ADB project team should also discuss the details of the M&E plan in the PAM with the stakeholders and agree on any necessary revisions or additions. In these discussions, it is helpful for the project team to (i) explain and confirm monitoring and reporting requirements including report formats and timelines; (ii) confirm data collection methodologies and sources, as these may

---

[20] For detailed guidance see ADB. 2017. *Impact Evaluation of Development Interventions: A Practical Guide*. Manila. https://www.adb.org/sites/default/files/publication/392376/impact-evaluation-development-interventions-guide.pdf.

[21] For an overview of tools and data collection methods and their application to ADB-financed operations consult Appendix II of ADB. 2012. *Handbook on Poverty and Social Analysis: A Working Document*. Manila. https://www.adb.org/sites/default/files/institutional-document/33763/files/handbook-poverty-social-analysis.pdf.

need to be updated or further specified; and (iii) ensure M&E systems and resources are in place, including clear assignment of responsibility for data collection and reporting. If adequate systems are not in place, a clear plan should be developed to establish them.

Using the design and monitoring framework for project monitoring. The DMF provides the results-focused structure for project monitoring. ADB review missions, including the in-depth midterm review, assess whether the project's outputs are being delivered or if adjustments are required to ensure that the outcome is likely to be achieved. The borrower's progress reports should provide the same analysis. Where necessary, remedial measures with an action plan are agreed between ADB and the borrower (Box 21).

Any adjustments to outputs, output indicators, activities, and risks and critical assumptions as well as further specification of the outcome and outcome indicators are attached to the back-to-office report of the review mission, reflected in a revised DMF, and transferred to the project progress report (PPR) (footnote 19). The ADB project team prepares a PPR in e-Operations at least quarterly throughout the project implementation period. Preparing the PPR includes rating the project's progress using five indicators, including progress in delivering DMF output targets.[22] The PPR also includes the value of results achieved to date for each DMF output indicator, progress on the completion of activities, and any updates to risks and critical assumptions. From the midterm review onward, progress toward achieving the outcome indicators is also reported, as relevant, based on when data can be collected.

Changing the design and monitoring framework after project approval. Adjusting the DMF is critical to ensure it remains a relevant monitoring and evaluation tool. The DMF should be adjusted when needed to reflect changing circumstances and project environments so that the intended project

Box 21: Tips for Using the Design and Monitoring Framework as a Project Management and Supervision Tool

Effectively using the design and monitoring framework as a project management and supervision tool entails

(i) regularly monitoring and reporting on progress against indicator targets;

(ii) explaining and discussing variance (actual performance vs. targets);

(iii) identifying problems by flagging issues and risks, and creating and assigning an action plan to address them; and

(iv) reviewing the design and monitoring framework and adjusting it when needed to reflect changing circumstances and project environments.

Source: Asian Development Bank. 2013. Bank Policy on Project Performance Management System. *Operations Manual*. OM Section J1/BP. Manila.

outcome can be achieved. Any revisions to the DMF should be agreed by ADB and the borrower, and clearly documented and explained in the approval memorandum for change in scope or in the Board paper, if prepared. A revised DMF showing the changes is attached to these documents. The revised DMF clearly identifies where content in the latest approved DMF has been added, deleted, or amended. It is recommended to use the DMF template for additional financing. All approved changes should be reflected in e-Operations to ensure the next PPR is based on the updated DMF.

The DMF can be revised at any point during project implementation (Box 22). Changes should be made as soon as the need becomes apparent and ideally

---

during the early stages of implementation. A project's midpoint is also an opportune time. By bringing together an experienced and complementary team of mission members, the midterm review mission is well-placed to conduct an in-depth assessment with the borrower of whether the project is likely to achieve its outcome and outputs on time and within budget, and to consider whether the outcome and output targets remain relevant in the current project context and environment.[23] It is often helpful to hire an M&E consultant to support the midterm review.

Major vs. minor change in scope. A major change in scope materially alters or fundamentally affects the approved scope and project outcome. A minor change in scope is defined as any change with respect to an ADB-approved project that does not result in a major change. A minor change includes changes to project outputs, percentage weights assigned to output performance indicators, or output performance targets.[24]

Additional financing. Additional financing requires a revised DMF as part of the approval documentation. The RRP for additional financing restates the project's

---

> ### Box 22: When to Revise the Design and Monitoring Framework
>
> When considering whether to revise the design and monitoring framework (DMF), project teams must respect the DMF's dual purpose as a tool for project management and for accountability. When performance is falling behind target, remedial actions should be taken to put the project back on track. The DMF should not be revised solely to change targets because the project risks not achieving them. DMF revisions should reflect adjustments in project design undertaken to respond to a change in the project context or environment in order to maximize the development results achieved.

---

results and indicators and clarifies whether they have changed on account of the additional financing. It is expected that a request to add significant additional financing to scale up and/or restructure an ongoing project will entail changes to the outputs and/or outcomes of the project's DMF. The RRP for additional financing contains a revised DMF that compares the ongoing project (before additional financing) with the project with additional financing.

C. Completion

The main objectives of a completion report are to evaluate performance in order to enhance transparency and accountability and to learn from operational experience to improve the design and implementation of ongoing and future projects. The completion report for sovereign operations presents the self-evaluation of overall project performance and rates the project's success based on an assessment using the core criteria of relevance, effectiveness, efficiency, and sustainability. This is complemented by an assessment using the non-core criteria of development impacts, ADB and cofinancier performance, and borrower and executing agency performance. For TA, the completion report assesses the development results and rates TA performance using the core criteria of relevance, effectiveness, and efficiency. This is complemented by an assessment of the likelihood that the TA results will be sustained.

The DMF serves as the basis for the completion report prepared by ADB and the borrower. It informs the assessment on most of the evaluation criteria, but especially the project's effectiveness rating, which is based on an assessment of the achievement of the outputs and outcome based on targets in the DMF, including any revisions approved during implementation (footnote 19). Thus, the most recently approved DMF forms the basis for preparing the completion report and subsequent independent

---

[23] Project Administration Instructions 6.02 describes the functions of projects administration missions. (ADB. 2018. Project Administration Missions. *Project Administration Instructions*. PAI 6.02. Manila. https://www.adb.org/documents/project-administration-instructions.).

[24] Change-in-scope processes, including approval authority and reporting, are detailed in the Project Administration Instructions 5.02 (ADB. 2018. Change in Loan Projects. *Project Administration Instructions*. PAI 5.02. Manila. https://www.adb.org/documents/project-administration-instructions.).

evaluations, such as project performance evaluation reports, and the original DMF is referenced if relevant.[25]

The completion report for sovereign investment projects (PCR) is circulated within 12 months after the financial closing date of the project. The completion report for TA is circulated within 6 months of the financial closing date of the TA.[26] Outcome-level indicators and targets in the DMF should be set considering these circulation timelines to ensure outcome data are available to include in the completion report.

For detailed guidance on preparing a PCR, consult ADB's *Guidelines for the Evaluation of Public Sector Operations* (footnote 25). For guidance on preparing a TA completion report, consult ADB's *Technical Assistance Completion Report Validation Guidelines.*[27]

---

[25] ADB. 2016. *Guidelines for the Evaluation of Public Sector Operations.* Manila. https://www.adb.org/sites/default/files/institutional-document/32516/guidelines-evaluation-public-sector.pdf.

[26] Procedures for various modalities and financing, in particular for policy-based lending and the MFF, differ and are outlined in Project Administration Instructions 6.07 (ADB. 2019. Project Completion Report and Extended Annual Review Report. *Project Administration Instructions.* PAI 6.07. Manila. https://www.adb.org/documents/project-administration-instructions.).

[27] Independent Evaluation Department. 2020. *Technical Assistance Completion Report Validation Guidelines.* Manila: ADB. https://www.adb.org/sites/default/files/institutional-document/528046/tcr-validation-guidelines.pdf.

Using the DMF

www.ingramcontent.com/pod-product-compliance
Lightning Source LLC
Chambersburg PA
CBHW051657210326
41518CB00026B/2619